PERCEPTIONOLOGY® 101

Tangible interpersonal communication practices that will:

Develop your network

Expand your career opportunities &

Enhance your leadership capability because…

How you are perceived is your Reality™

Donald Wayne McLeod

Upper Front Cover Photo Credit: Karen Brown McLeod

Lower Front Cover Photo Credit: Kasey Samuel Adams Photography.

P.O. Box 413   Hiram, Ohio 44234

www.kaseysamueladamsphotography.com

PERCEPTIONOLOGY® 101

Published by: CreateSpace Independent Publishing Platform

Copyright © 2014 -2015 Donald Wayne McLeod

www.PERCEPTIONOLOGY.com

ISBN-13: 978-1503056183

To my wife, Karen Lynne, the best thing to ever happen to me.

Acknowledgement

A special and sincere "Thank You" to Debbie Loughry who listened to countless hours of my lectures, helped organize my thoughts and never stopped encouraging me to finish writing this book.

A Personal Narrative Essay

By: Heather Spikes (age 17)

What Leadership Means to Me

A leader can be defined as someone with a higher position that controls others; or it can also mean being a good role model, making a difference, and inspiring others to make a change. Great leaders must carry themselves in a professional manner that others can look up to. Their words, more importantly, should match their actions. Leaders need to be able to see a problem, want to resolve it, and then execute a plan to make that change possible.

Accordingly, a leader should be able to inspire that passion and desire to want to make a difference in others. Leadership is all about setting a good example for others and being a person of action, not just words. An influential role model, who knows what it means to be a leader, is Donald Wayne McLeod, and he changed my life forever.

In the summer, following my sophomore year of high school, I was selected to participate in a week long program called Learn About Business (LAB) and a yearlong program called Leadership Lake County, which is where I first met Mr. McLeod. After hours of lectures were given every day, the room still lit up when, seven-foot-tall, Donald Wayne McLeod walked in; giving his "Best Hello."

Donald Wayne McLeod is a self-made business man and is the creator and developer of PERCEPTIONOLOGY® which is a practice that focuses on business and life etiquette so that one can be perceived as the best reflection of themselves. This extraordinary man created a 21st century themed skills class that he has been perfecting for the last six years while speaking to thousands of high school and college students as well as business professionals. As a prominent role model in my journey through LAB and Leadership Lake County, Donald Wayne taught me how to become the confident, successful woman I know I am capable of being.

In modern society, judging others and ourselves becomes second nature. Everybody is being perceived 24/7/365. That is the reason Donald Wayne teaches business associates and students how to leave a positive lasting impression.

It all starts with our "Best Hello." Since first impressions are key, starting off with an energetic and sincere "hello" gives you an advantage over any competitor. Through his practice, Donald Wayne addresses the importance of meeting and greeting potential business connections in a professional manner, and it starts with remembering their name. In a program of hundreds of people, he knew every student, faculty, and guest's first and last name.

He teaches the skill of listening and asking questions because being truly interested in others will benefit you personally, professionally, and financially. By making that investment of your time and effort, the connections you make will, in return, make an investment in you and your future.

Donald Wayne also gives lectures about presenting yourself as a professional and selling yourself. The famous saying is "actions speak louder than words" so from body language to public speaking, he prepared me to enter the business world at the tender age of sixteen, with more refined skills than many CEOs of multimillion dollar companies.

Throughout my time in Leadership Lake County and LAB I felt challenged to utilize the skills I learned from Donald Wayne who constantly reminded me of them each program day. I never really felt like I fit in anywhere until he showed me the potential I had to thrive in this program and in life. Every program day I greeted and thanked the speakers for their time, asked questions, and most importantly, networked by asking for their business cards. Something so simple set me so far apart from my peers. In return I was being offered recommendation letters and internships left and right, opportunities I never would have had if I did not put myself out there.

When I attended the Lake County Communicators Christmas Luncheon with Bob Ulas, a prominent leader in the Lake County Ohio Marketing Program, I was the only teenager there, but I presented myself as a young adult and impressed everyone around me because Donald Wayne had critiqued and perfected my public speaking skills.

As an opinionated young woman, I often had thoughts on the topic at hand, but would keep quiet because of intimidation of my peers. With his help, I stand tall and proud with my chin held high, projecting my voice across the room for all to hear while engaging them with eye contact. My confidence has skyrocketed and as a result I am no longer afraid to get up in front of my class and recite that speech I worked so hard on because I now know how to properly execute a public speech.

The most important lesson Donald Wayne taught me was that I have the power to influence other people and the ability to change the world. One of his favorite teaching techniques is sharing the statistics of getting a hole-in-one or winning the lottery, but we have all already won our one life lottery. This reminds me to be grateful for all that I have, including the opportunity to have a mentor like Donald Wayne. From day one at LAB to graduation a year later from Leadership Lake County, I knew his lessons would be with me for the rest of my life, most likely as a successful billionaire because of these skills.

He once told me that he was willing to invest in me and invest in my future, because he believed in me. He also told me I stood out from the crowd because I took what he said to heart, and that I was capable of doing anything I put my mind to, even if it meant ruling the world because I have the passion and drive to do so. He taught me to make the best out of every opportunity because another may not come along. So every day I take the chance given to me.

I know that the day I walk across the stage to receive my first Emmy or the day my novel becomes a New York Best Seller, I will give Mr. McLeod the most sincere "thank you" for his investment in my success. As Gandhi once said, "Be the change you wish to see in the world," and because of the help of Donald Wayne McLeod, I will change the world.

CONTENTS

Introduction

Every day, within seconds, everyone you come into contact with subconsciously perceives you on a multitude of levels. They take into account your appearance, your posture, your language, your manners, your smile, your handshake, your eye contact, and other behaviors. They may never actually speak to you, but they perceive you as being confident, friendly, interesting, and honest; or perhaps they decide that you're insecure, hostile, boring or dishonest. How valuable would it be to know how people truly perceive you?

Ironically, most people are not willing to share their honest perceptions of you, with you, especially if their opinions are negative. Think about it: when was the last time you told someone that he/she exhibited a certain characteristic or had a particular behavior that made you perceive him/her negatively? For example, the person might have a weak handshake, or doesn't look you in the eye when shaking your hand. Perhaps he/she doesn't look you in the eye while speaking to you, or never stops talking.

Any one of these behaviors could possibly influence a potential client to perceive you in a negative way. He/she observes your mannerisms, forms an opinion and neglects to mention it to the one person who would benefit the most; you. Unfortunately, that same person will have no problem telling any number of others about this negative perception of you.

Even worse, this negative perception could result in lost opportunities. For example, clients won't say to you, "Are you ever going to stop talking and listen to me?" They will most likely allow you to drone on until frustration sets in and they realize they would rather be hit by a bus than do business with you. And how fast do you think their destructive perception of you is going to spread? That's right, like wildfire. Instead of having conversations with others, you now become the negative topic of conversation. The fact is, without knowing the truth of how others truly perceive you, you are condemned to remain unchanged, forever repeating the same critical mistakes that cost you money, business opportunities and friends.

In your personal life you need to work on your relationships with your parents, your family, your friends and your teachers, among others. In your professional life, you need to develop personal relationships with your clients, your fellow employees, your superiors and other professionals. These interpersonal relationships provide the fuel that drives your life.

Sadly, the lack of interpersonal communication skills in current society has become very evident. I have watched as grown men and women walked up and rudely interrupted a conversation in ways that even a five-year old has enough manners not to do. Every day people have greeted me half-heartedly, with weak handshakes, no eye contact and little energy, and expected me to do business with them. Often the person I just met didn't remember my name. Observing people treating each other as if they're unimportant and interchangeable has made me want to yell, "Hello people; if you'll put a little effort into changing your attitudes and behaviors, it will benefit you!"

In response to what I observed, I started confronting business people about their lack of professionalism, not in a mean or sarcastic way but on a genuine and personal level. My goal wasn't to embarrass them, but rather to inform them about how I perceived them based on their behaviors. If a businessman did not stand to greet me I would ask, "Why aren't you standing? Do you not care to meet me?" Each time, he would get to his feet embarrassed and apologetic, because he knew it was the right thing to do. If someone didn't look me in the eye while shaking my hand I would call him/her on it. While your hand is in another's hand, your eyes should be on his/her eyes… period. This is a simple two-second gesture that communicates sincerity.

What pleasantly surprised me was the response I received from these people. The majority of them responded positively to my feedback. They were actually glad that I told them how I perceived their actions because no one else was willing to do so. They understood that I was bringing it to their attention because I cared about them as individuals. They appreciated my candor and expressed the intention to change their ways. Many wanted to know what else I could teach them.

The simple things I mention here are just the tip of the iceberg. There is a lot more to share on how to form productive, meaningful, and lasting personal and professional relationships. Your success can only begin, however, with the understanding that you have a great deal of control over how people perceive you. Furthermore, the way others perceive you will impact your life much more than you realize. It will determine your earning potential and your ability to make, and more importantly, keep friends. It will also directly influence whether people identify with you, and how others receive your thoughts, concepts and ideas. More importantly, their perceptions will determine how much others will be willing to do for you. And since you deal with people virtually every day of your life in many different ways, these perceptions can affect every aspect of your life.

Conversely, you have the power to positively impact the life of every person you know. You can strengthen your relationships by encouraging and empowering others. You possess unique qualities, and your words and comments can be meaningful to those who perceive you as someone who is genuinely interested in them.

I felt compelled to write this handbook for several reasons. First, I have been blessed with an innate ability to connect with people; this has helped me teach others. Secondly, I have personally experienced positive results by applying the concepts you will be reading about. In order to achieve my ultimate goals in life I need to inspire others to help me, and they are responding. Why? As my wife has said more than once, "You don't practice what you preach, you preach what you practice." Finally, I feel a deep responsibility to awaken in you the amazing power that you possess.

I want to empower you with techniques that will enable you to interact with people on an unprecedented level. My goal is for you to be able to speak to anyone, at any time, about anything, and to be perceived in a positive light. When you want to express your thoughts, concepts and ideas, I want you to be able to express yourself so you will be heard and taken seriously. I want those thoughts and ideas to land on listening ears, so that you are understood as clearly as possible.

But first, you need to understand that to accomplish these gains, you must learn critical 'people skills' and employ them every day. If you want to be heard, you need to first listen. If you want to be loved, you must first love. By giving, you receive; and when you are truly interested in others, *you* benefit. Although these seem like simple truths, the common sense techniques that are derived from them are amazingly powerful. They will enable you to live a happier life and realize your full potential.

Take your time reading this book. Since there is a lot of information contained in these pages you need to allow it to sink in one bite at a time. However, you will quickly discover how these tangible interpersonal communication principles will dramatically change the way you interact with others and how others begin interacting with you. Your network and self-confidence will grow exponentially and your power to influence will skyrocket.

Start applying one lesson at a time in your own professional and/or personal life. Some of the techniques may seem odd to you at first, but try them and see how they impact those you communicate with. Add some notes at the end of each section on what happened as a result; these will personalize the lessons and provide thoughts for continued improvement. As you notice positive results, continue to incorporate them into your daily interactions.

I know you will find this book helpful to you as you continue to increase your interpersonal communication skills. I truly believe that if you put these basic concepts and techniques into practice it will benefit you personally, spiritually, professionally and financially.

Good Morning,

Donald Wayne McLeod

"So, let us summon a new spirit of patriotism, of
responsibility, where each of us resolves to pitch in and work
harder and look over not only ourselves, but each other."

~ Barack Obama

Acknowledge Others

If you want to build relationships and increase your business and
networking opportunities, make the effort to acknowledge those around
you. It will not only benefit you; it will separate you from the crowd.
The definition of the word 'acknowledge' is "to recognize as genuine so
as to give validity." How often do we acknowledge or validate those
around us? The answer is, not enough, or not at all. Perhaps this is
because no one is acknowledging us, either. Think about how many
people pass you by on a daily basis without even as a smile, eye contact
or a hello. It would be hard to say because we have grown so accustomed
to being ignored. We go through our daily lives seemingly invisible to
others.

Start acknowledging those around you, and watch how it will benefit
you. For example, I make it a point to acknowledge and thank all
veterans I see for their service to our country. If you are looking for
veterans, you will see them all around you. Perhaps they are wearing a
pin, hat or jacket with their military affiliation. Be aware of the freedoms
you possess today that were dearly paid for, and thank and acknowledge
these men and women for the sacrifices they made for these freedoms.
Then consciously watch their reaction and see that your comments
matter. You matter.

In addition to veterans, I want you to acknowledge everyone around you.
I won't order a cup of coffee at Starbucks until I look the person behind
the counter in the eye and say hello to them. I want to acknowledge them
as a person and not just a generic food service worker. Try it the next
time you're at the deli, dry cleaners, movie theater or gas station. Take
two extra seconds and acknowledge the person behind the counter, and
watch how you separate yourself from the crowd. This will help you
appreciate your amazing ability to validate others.

Making it yours

Speaking of gas stations, when you fuel up do you go to *a* gas station or *your* gas station? The difference might seem unimportant, but it may make a huge difference in how you are treated. **A** gas station is a place where no one acknowledges you. **Your** gas station is a place where you acknowledge the people working there and they acknowledge you.

As soon as I set foot in my gas station, the employees acknowledge me with an energetic hello and call me by name. They continually go out of their way to service my needs, and ask me how my day is going. As I leave, they always give me a great goodbye using eye contact. I know that this is not the normal way people are treated at a gas station, but it can be. Let me take you back a few months.

When I first started using *my* gas station, no one acknowledged me at all. Interaction between the customers and employees was nonexistent and there was a perceptible feeling of negativity throughout the establishment. One particularly cold, dark winter morning I studied customers standing silently in line at the register. Their heads were down as they stood six people deep. I could hear the attendant complaining about working there. There was no energy being exchanged between the attendant and customers, and vice versa. No one was acknowledging anyone. It was a depressing situation, as you can imagine.

Can just one person change the attitude of an entire store? Absolutely; but it won't be accomplished by walking up to someone and saying, "Your attitude stinks." What you can do is acknowledge the attendant and get his name, as I did with Matthew Anthony Tracz (you will read more about this concept in a later segment).

The next four times I went into the store, I acknowledged Matthew Anthony using his first and middle names, while also reminding him of my name. I would ask him questions about himself and listen to his replies. What I was doing was building the foundation of our relationship. After building a rapport with him I was able to address the issue at hand. I asked him if he realized that his attitude impacted every one of his customers, and that a smile and a positive comment from him would go a long way.

I was simply acknowledging him and his ability to influence everyone he met. He was very receptive at this point, and said that he'd never really thought about it. I said, "Well, think about it, because you really do matter. You are often the first person people come in contact with during their day, and by simply acknowledging them you can set a positive tone for their entire day."

He said he would become more consciously aware of his own attitude and of the importance of acknowledging his customers, and he has. In fact, he has helped the rest of the staff understand this very basic but effective concept. It was remarkable to witness the positive change in how the staff and customers interacted. The staff now acknowledge their customers and the customers naturally acknowledge them back. There are smiles where there once were frowns, and there is positive energy where there once was none.

Everyone motivates
When people ask me if I consider myself to be a motivational speaker, I tell them this story:

> A motivational speaker once pulled a $20 bill out of his pocket and asked his audience, "Would anyone like this $20 bill?" Of course, a lot of hands went up. The speaker then crumpled the $20 bill into a ball and asked, "Would anyone still like this $20 bill?" Once again a lot of hands went up. The speaker then dropped the crumpled $20 bill onto the floor, stepped on it, then picked it up and asked, "Would anyone still like this $20 bill?" Once again hands went up, because everyone knows that the value of the now-dirtier $20 bill had not diminished. The moral of the speaker's story was; sometimes you will have bad days. You may not be looking or feeling your best, but you are still worth your full value, just like the $20 bill.

However, my personal moral to that story is: everyone can be a 'motivational speaker.' The next time you meet someone who may be wearing dirty clothes, is speaking broken English, has lots of tattoos, green hair or whatever else it is that makes you perceive them as different, acknowledge them. Get rid of your prejudices and preconceived perceptions about who that person is, and see their value as a person.

You have no idea who you will meet today who could change your life forever. How many of you are married or in love? Did you see it coming? What a difference a day makes. One day, and one person can change your entire life.

APPLY THIS IN YOUR LIFE:
 Acknowledge those around you on a daily basis. The next time you're in line for service, remember to acknowledge the person waiting on you. Take two seconds to let them know you see them as a person who deserves respect. Call them by name and thank them with eye contact and watch how they appreciate you. Remember, in order to be acknowledged we must first acknowledge others.

Track when you practiced these techniques and how it benefitted you.

_____

_____

_____

_____

_____

_____

_____

_____

_____

_____

_____

_____

> "No one cares what you know
> until they know that you care."
>
> ~ *Benjamin Franklin*

Be Truly Interested

One of the most important underlying principles of this book is the fact that becoming truly interested in others benefits you personally, professionally and financially. When you become genuinely interested in others, everything else you are about to learn will fall naturally into place. If you want to build stronger interpersonal relationships with your clients, coworkers, friends, and perhaps more importantly your family, then consciously focus on engaging with them.

Once you become truly interested in others, you will find yourself wanting to employ the interpersonal communication techniques found in this book. For example, you will want to provide their 'best hello' of the day and will want to remember their names. You will want to engage them in conversation, and will begin to talk less and listen more. You will stop trying to 'outdo' their stories and will start to realize your own ability to encourage others. All of these changes will lead you to a greater respect and appreciation of other people's opinions. In the end, you will understand that by giving you will receive, and by helping others achieve their goals you are actually achieving your own.

Self-absorption: bad for business
It always amazes me how self-centered professional adults can be when they interact at networking functions. They often approach me with their business cards extended, then tell me who they are, what they do, where they live and what their company does, all before even asking for my name. Don't be one of those people. If you want people to be interested in what you do, first be interested in what *they* do.

Typically, when someone does hold his/her card in front of my face, I take it. After a few minutes I will approach the person again and ask, "Can you tell me my name?" They almost always can't. As I had perceived during my first interaction with that person, he/she wasn't interested in meeting me, only in *selling* me on their story. I'm sure many of you have had a similar experience. If they can't remember my name, I hand their card back to them. Interestingly, although they are initially embarrassed, these networkers usually thank me for revealing this flawed behavior to them because they had not realized how they were being perceived.

A word to the wise: you don't want your business card in someone's hand the first two minutes you're talking with him/her; you want it there for the *last* two minutes of the conversation, and preferably after they ask you, "What do you do?" When you engage others and show interest in them first, it sets you apart from the crowd. They will naturally ask you what you do because they're pleased that you cared about them. Now, both you and your conversational partner are listening as you hand him/her your card.

Helping others helps you
When the opportunity presents itself to speak to professional networking groups, I tell the members they need to check their egos at the door and care about each other. All too often participants come into such settings with their own agenda. They're not thinking how they can help other members of their group; they're only thinking about how the organization can help them, or are focused on their own problems. Consequently, I have watched members of such organizations walk into a room so obviously depressed that their body language is screaming it out, but no one is listening.

Early on in my speaking career I was scheduled to speak to a networking group that had 30 members. The day I presented, only six members showed up. One man in particular walked in late, looking like he had just run over his child's puppy. His head was down, his shoulders hunched, and he was practically dragging his briefcase into the room. I was stunned that not one person got up to greet him. Not one person cared enough to ask him, "What's the matter?" Everyone there had his/her own agenda, and it showed. When I spoke to the group I said, "After witnessing how you treat each other I am surprised even six of you show up here." The group disbanded three months later, which was no surprise to me because I could see the writing on the wall.

I believe that for a networking organization to successfully optimize its membership potential, the members need to be truly interested in each other. They need to enter the meeting thinking, "What can I do for everyone else? How can I help support and encourage each of the people in this group?" Imagine; if everyone in the group did this, then the entire organization would be working on *your* business. Now *that's* networking and collaboration!

APPLY THIS IN YOUR LIFE:
No one cares what you know until they know that you care. Start taking the time to truly listen to others. Show people that you care by focusing on them as you approach, and by greeting them with energy. Become truly interested in those around you and watch how it positively impacts you personally, professionally and financially.

Track when you practiced these techniques and how it benefitted you.

_____

_____

_____

_____

_____

_____

_____

_____

"Silence is one of the great arts of conversation."

~ Marcus Tullius Cicero

Converse

I was hired by a national bank to work with 20 branch managers on the topic of engaging their customers. I was going to be meeting with them over a dozen times. After the first meeting, I called ten of them by phone and held a 45-minute conversation with each, in which I learned many details about each person. When I returned to the bank for the second meeting I referenced those conversations. I was able to address all ten managers and tell their coworkers something personal about each of them.

I shared with everyone that one of their team members was one of 19 children, and how that was a story in itself. I was able to mention that another manager loved horses and that she owned four of them. I shared her story of trying to round up her horses at two o'clock in the morning during a driving rain and lightning storm, while still in her pajamas.

I continued to share other stories I had learned from my phone conversations, such as that one of the managers hosted the family Christmas at her house while Thanksgiving was held at her sister's house. During this story-telling I asked each of the people I had spoken with, "We had a great conversation didn't we?" They all agreed that we had wonderful conversations.

I continued down the line, speaking about their children, how many years they had been at the bank and where each of them was from originally. I mentioned brothers and sisters by name. I was able to mention certain achievements, honors and awards that each of them had received. I again asked the ten of them, "We had a great conversation, didn't we?" Again, they all agreed that we had had marvelous conversations. At this point, I turned to the group and asked, "Can any of you tell me anything about me?"

Silence filled the room. The group had that deer-in-the-headlights look. They tried to tell me things that they learn about me from our first meeting together, but none of the ten could tell me anything new that they had learned during our phone conversation. All ten agreed that we had wonderful conversations, but not one of them could tell me anything about me – because they had never asked me anything.

There is a great irony here. All 10 managers agreed that we had wonderful conversations, never realizing that in reality the converse was true. There was no conversation going on at all – it was all one-sided. I was simply listening to them and asking questions about what they were saying. I can't tell you how many times people say," I can't believe I'm telling you this." I can believe it because I am actually listening to them. People will tell you anything if they believe you're sincerely listening.

Listening gives you control
The best part of being a listener is that you control the conversation. You are directing where the conversation will go. For example, the story I mentioned above about the woman going out to round up her horses in the middle of a thunderstorm didn't just happen; I made it happen. Knowing she had horses, I asked her how they reacted during storms. She told me they were very skittish. I then asked her if she ever had a hard time rounding them up. She then told me about the storm incident.

As I tried to picture what she was telling me I was able to continue to ask her questions to fill in the 'color.' I asked if it was hard to see in the storm; she told me yes, and at one point the horses seemed to disappear because between flashes they moved to the other side of the pasture so they weren't where she was looking the next time she could see. I said it must have been surreal only seeing flashes of reality; she said yes, it was, and added that her senses were on overload. She shared how afraid she was when one lightning flash revealed her horses galloping straight at her on their way to the barn.

She confirmed that the rain was torrential and had soaked her to the bone and that she fell three times and actually dove into the mud once during the ordeal. And no, she couldn't go back to bed even after a warm shower because her adrenaline was still pumping.

This was a great story, but I made it happen. I showed an interest in her and an interest in her story. I wasn't just listening in black and white – I was recreating the experience with her. More importantly, I as the listener controlled this conversation, and was able to hear the parts of the story I wanted to hear. I was able to hone in on particular statements and ask questions that helped me understand more clearly the emotions that were running through her and fill in all the details that would help me understand what she had gone through.

Can you see how this manager believed we had a great conversation? Wouldn't you have thought you had a great conversation if you could tell a great story in such glorious detail because someone wanted to hear it? If you think about it, each and every one of us may be more interesting than any movie, if you just take the time to ask the questions and listen to the answers. Is that how you converse with someone? Do you really care what they're trying to tell you? Are you asking them questions to make sure you understand them and show them you are sincerely interested?

Talk, then reverse

I will often tell people, after talking to them for an hour, that if they are talking for more than five minutes they need to shut up and ask a question. The very definition of the word converse means reversed, opposite and contrary. What that means is, you talk and then reverse it, do the opposite and listen, which is what *convers*ation is all about.

Please hold on to this thought: *if you want to be considered a great conversationalist, first learn how to be a great listener.* Just as in the example I just gave you above, when you intensely listen to others they will think they had a wonderful conversation and that you are a great conversationalist. People will even walk away from you thinking there is something special about you because you actually listen. This, again, will help you stand out in their memory.

If you're thinking of starting a conversation, here is a short list of topics people love to talk about: their kids, their job, their spouse, their hobbies and their passions. You get the picture; they like to talk about themselves, so let them. Just remember, as the listener you can control the conversation, so direct it in a way that is of interest to you.

Here's another example of directing the conversation to your preferences. I was speaking to an older gentleman who was bragging about his grandson. It's a fact of life that all grandparents think their grandchildren are the greatest things since sliced bread. Since I didn't want to hear the same old story, I redirected the conversation by asking him, "What were you like as a kid?" "Oh I was a hell-raiser," he said. Great, I thought to myself, there is a story here. "Give me an example of getting in trouble," I said.

He told me he attended a Catholic grade school. One day, during his lunchtime, he went out into the nearby field and collected grasshoppers in his empty milk box. When he returned to the classroom he started throwing the grasshoppers at the nun as she walked past him. Back then the nuns wore a habit that covered everything but their face and hands. The habit included a long veil that ran all the way down their backs to the floor. He told me that those veils were better than Velcro® as far as the grasshoppers were concerned. He was able to toss some grasshoppers over ten feet and have them stick to her. The nun kept talking to the class even though the students, seeing what was happening, started laughing. He told me he had over eleven grasshoppers affixed to her veil before one of them crawled over the top of her cowl and started staring down at her. At this point the sister started freaking out and wanted to know where the grasshopper came from. Within a second, he said, every student in the room was pointing at him.

"Great story," I said, "Now tell me what the detention was like." His punishment was to arrive on Saturday and move all the desks out into the hallway, throw cornmeal on the floor, and shuffle the meal around with his feet, which was how they polished asbestos floors in the day. He then had to sweep up all the cornmeal and do it all over again. Since the janitor was coming to realign the desks the following morning, he did not need to put the desks back into the room. After his detention, as he was leaving to walk home, he doubled backed and quietly lined up the desks in the hallway across the hall, in front of a closed classroom door with a nun still inside the classroom. As you may have imagined, she couldn't open the door out into the hallway.

What he essentially did was lock a nun in her classroom for six hours. With no way to contact anyone (pre cell phone and computer era), she finally escaped by climbing out of a window that tilted out. The story is even funnier when you realize that this was back when nuns wore long habits that came down to their shoes, with long sleeves and head gear that only allowed you to see their faces. Thinking about that story still makes me smile.

This was a much more entertaining story than what I would have heard otherwise, but I had to make it happen. And yes, I found out what the consequences of this prank were from the school and from his father, but that is another story.

APPLY THIS IN YOUR LIFE:
The next time you are in a conversation with someone, remember it is a two-way street. Talk, and then conversely, listen. Ask questions as if there was going to be a test. Decide what part of the story you would like to know more about, and ask follow-up questions related to that part. Watch how the speaker gladly fills in the missing pieces to bring the story to life. You control the conversation, and this can be both powerful and extremely entertaining!

Track when you practiced these techniques and how it benefitted you.

_____

_____

_____

_____

_____

_____

_____

_____

_____

_____

_____

_____

_____

_____

_____

_____

_____

"If you would win a man to your cause,
first convince him that you are his sincere friend."

~ Abraham Lincoln

Do It In Reverse

What makes us want to help someone? What makes someone want to help us? I believe the answer is in the quality of the relationship between the helper and the person receiving help. Only when we have treated someone with respect and have appreciated who he/she truly is, do we create a reason for that person to help us; not because they have to, but because they sincerely want to help.

Let me tell you a story about a man I will call David, with whom I was constantly bumping heads while operating a high-end remodeling company. David worked for one of the two major plumbing supply companies in my area. I was glad he worked for the one we used less often, because working with David was a pain. Whenever I needed to use David's company, he would take my order and inevitably mess it up.

For example, the sink might come in the wrong color, or it had the wrong number of holes drilled in it. Maybe the drain plug was missing, or the faucets were not the correct style. Some of the pieces wouldn't arrive on time, or sometimes not arrive at all. This became quite bothersome, since I was trying to finish projects on time and these issues were forcing me to postpone projects for weeks or a month.

Whenever I had someone pick up any materials that were ordered from David, I would instruct them to open the package and inspect it to make sure it was correct. Once they were sure it was the right item I would make sure they checked it for defects. It was becoming such a hassle to deal with him. If I returned an item, it would take countless phone calls to David to assure that my account was credited, and that didn't occur until months later.

Time for a showdown

You can imagine my relief when I heard that the company David worked for had fired him. That relief didn't last, because the other plumbing supply company that we used even more often hired David! Now I found myself having to deal with David even more than before. I decided I was going to put an end to this chaos once and for all. My life had to get easier.

The 'showdown' took place in David's showroom, and I made sure there were several of his co-workers standing around within earshot. When David saw me coming, I could see a look of terror in his eyes. He knew I was going to let him have it.

When he asked me why I was there I said in a loud voice, "I came to apologize to you for my attitude." Now I could see the look of confusion in his eyes. "What?" he said. "I came to apologize to you for my attitude," I said again. "I know nothing is easy and that you are doing your best. I understand you take pride in your job and that you really are trying your best to service my company. I apologize for being upset and demanding and from this day forward you will see a change in my attitude towards you." I thanked him for his patience with me and said that I looked forward to working with him in the future. With that, I shook his hand and walked out.

What do you think happened after that interaction? Just what I had hoped would happen; not only did I stop having problems with David, but he actually became a pleasure to work with. Everything started arriving not only as ordered, but also on time. In the rare case of a returned item, David would call me the next day to tell me when it would be credited back to my account. He still treated everyone else in a less than professional manner, but he could not do enough to help me, and that made my job and my life a whole lot easier.

This complete change in David's service efforts happened because I validated him in front of his peers. I challenged him to do his job to the best of his ability and thanked him in advance for doing so. He couldn't help but rise to the occasion.

I gave David a reason to want to help me, and you have the capacity to do the same. Don't be afraid to validate a person that you are having problems with. It will benefit you tremendously.

APPLY THIS IN YOUR LIFE:
Your assignment is to pick someone with whom you have been having difficulty. It could be at work or at home. Give that person a reason to want to help you by beginning to treat them with respect and by validating them as a person. Watch them rise to the occasion and your expectations.

Track when you practiced these techniques and how it benefitted you.

_____

_____

_____

_____

_____

_____

_____

_____

_____

_____

_____

_____

_____

_____

_____

_____

"When you encourage others,
and you watch them become encouraged,
it will encourage you to encourage others."

~ Donald Wayne McLeod

Encourage Others

If you want to inspire others to help you achieve your goals, then encourage them to accomplish theirs. Once you realize that you have the ability to encourage all those around you, your self-worth and confidence will grow as well. People remember those who encourage them, and it still amazes me how one simple encouraging statement can change someone's life forever.

Early in my speaking career I was presenting a two-hour lecture to a group of business professionals. Four times during the lecture, one of the participants left and then returned. After the lecture I asked her why she kept leaving the session. She responded, "I am sick and have been throwing up all morning." When I asked her, "Why didn't you just go home?" She replied, "Because I didn't want to miss anything."

Talk about making my day. Talk about encouraging me. I knew right then and there that I could do this; I could speak for a living. You never know what you might say to someone today that will change his/her life forever, but it will. I am living proof of that, and I want to thank you, Linda Burnett Allen.

One of the greatest gifts we have as human beings is our ability to encourage one another. With a few simple words we can make someone's day, lighten their load or perhaps help them hold on to a dream. The problem is that we don't use it often enough. If I asked you when the last time was that someone truly encouraged you, it would probably take you some time to come up with an answer. However, the more important question is, when was the last time *you* sincerely encouraged *someone else*? Once again, you may find yourself struggling for an answer.

Encouragement close to home

Here is the real kick in the head. We don't need to look far to see someone who would benefit from our words of encouragement. In the office, at school, at the grocery store, and in our own homes, we see people on a daily basis who need that little bit of verbal support. Let that fact sink in, then ask yourself why you aren't encouraging these folks already. What does it take for you to encourage others besides a few moments of your time, a few choice words, and the desire to make a difference? The only other thing you need is to believe that what you say will matter.

To start the process, we need to take the focus off ourselves and pay attention to those around us who might need a positive word. For example, have you ever noticed how easy it is for us to encourage the children in our lives? We hang their artwork from our refrigerator doors. We attend basketball, soccer and baseball games to encourage their efforts. We attend recitals, plays and concert performances and tell them how great they were. These encouraging activities are natural to many of us because we instinctively understand the importance of encouraging young egos (we will discuss this further in the 'Kudos' section).

But what about the single mother of three working a full-time job and struggling to make ends meet; do you see the need to encourage her? How about co-workers whose children are ill, or whose parents are showing signs of dementia? How about your friend, who's been unemployed for over a year, or your neighbor who's losing his home? These are all examples that seem obvious, so how about the folks with not-so-obvious issues; those who are healthy and successful by all measures but are having a really bad day, are doubting themselves, or are tense and anxious because they are juggling a lot of responsibilities?

The fact is, human beings need the positive reinforcement of encouragement on occasion in order to reach their full potential. Did you know that heavyweight champion Mike Tyson had Steve "Crocodile" Fitch, whose only job was to continually make encouraging remarks to the Champ, constantly by his side? Imagine having someone continually encouraging you; the things you could achieve!

You may not have an encouraging force in your life at the present time, but you can change that by *being* that encouraging force for others. By offering support that changes the course of another's day, you may redirect your own as well. Start encouraging others on a daily basis and witness how the positive power of your words impacts them. You do realize who will benefit most from all of this, don't you...?

APPLY THIS IN YOUR LIFE:
Start using your ability to be an encourager, today. Recognize when someone needs to be acknowledged and encouraged. Start to offer sincere verbal support to others, and watch how your own sense of self-worth grows, along with your opportunities.

Track when you practiced these techniques and how it benefitted you.

_____

_____

_____

_____

_____

_____

_____

_____

_____

_____

_____

_____

_____

> "And what is a man without energy?
> Nothing- nothing at all."
>
> ~ *Mark Twain*

F ear – Not!

Perhaps you experience it when you walk into a room full of people you don't know. Maybe you feel it when you have to get up and talk in front of a crowd. Most of us deal with it when walking into a job interview. Some of us may experience it when we are preparing to visit a terminally ill friend. Fear is an intrinsic human emotion. We all feel it; but it's how we deal with it that defines each of us.

Fear can cripple your business and networking opportunities, and you never know when it will strike. For example, you are in a roomful of people when a facilitator asks everyone to introduce him or herself. Do you feel a knot in the pit of your stomach? Does your mind start to race with thoughts of how much you hate doing this? Do you worry about what to say? Whether to stand and address the group? Whether you might stumble over your words? Many people are more afraid of speaking in public than they are of death (!) Ironically, most of us 'speak in public' every day.

To stand or not to stand

I was waiting to address 35 entrepreneurs at a business start-up workshop. The facilitator said, "Let's go around the room and introduce ourselves." The rectangular tables were arranged in a large U shape, with the participants sitting on the outside of the U formation, facing in. I was sitting in the bottom middle of the U. The first person to my left at the top of the U began the introductions. He did not stand, and spoke with very little energy. He didn't make eye contact with those listening. I was watching with interest to see what impact his presentation would have on the rest of the participants.

I believe that in groups, the behavior of the first person affects those who follow. For example, if the first person had stood, he would have influenced others to stand to introduce themselves. Conversely, by not standing he also influenced others to follow suit. The second person remained seated and spoke with the same low energy while presenting himself. If you were the third person in line, what would you do? Think about it for a moment. The first two people didn't stand. I'm sure you've been in this type of situation and have felt discomfort or fear about what to do.

In this particular case, the third person also did not stand, and so the precedent was set. No one else even thought about standing until it was my turn. I stood up, looked everyone in the eye, and pronounced my name clearly and with energy. I stated my company's name and told them I was looking forward to presenting to them on how to build better relationships, not only with their clients but also with their employees. I then sat down. The next person in line was also presenting an hour lecture that day, but he did not stand to introduce himself. And so it continued around the rest of the U, with no one else standing to speak.

When the time came for my presentation, I started it out by asking for affirmation that everyone was here to learn how to start a new business. They all agreed with me. I then said, "You all want to start a new business, but you seem fearful of standing up and saying who you are and what you do. Do you realize that there were 35 potential clients in this room to whom you were presenting yourselves and your companies? Were you presenting yourselves in the best possible light?"

What would Trump do?

I then asked, "If Donald Trump was here, do you think he would have stood to introduce himself? I am confident that, not only would he have stood; he would have engaged you all with his eyes, expressed an interest in you, and addressed you all with energy. That's why he is Donald Trump."

It amazes me how many times people pass up an opportunity to introduce themselves to a group. Yes, I said *opportunity* for a reason. We all need to market our businesses, and ourselves, and to be remembered. We are our own best marketing tools and we need to take better advantage of this.

Even though McDonald's is on practically every other street corner, they still spend over one billion dollars a year in advertising just to keep their name in front of you. What are you doing to keep your name in front of your potential clients? When presenting yourself, your goal should be to get people to remember your name. You need to introduce yourself

31

professionally every time you have the chance so that people will start to remember who you are and what you do.

Presenting yourself in a professional manner is a skill that can be practiced and learned. Standing up is the first step, but it doesn't get the job done. Whether you're speaking to one person or a crowd, the same rules apply; look at everyone who's listening to you, act confident, bring energy, speak clearly and succinctly, and engage your listener(s).

FEAR is not what you think
I have a more powerful and positive use for the acronym FEAR: Fantastic Energy Always Ready.

When you are fearful, you are generating a lot of nervous energy (thoughts flying, feelings of fight or flight). This energy is pent up and needs an outlet. The next time you feel fear, use it to fuel your presentation or conversation. Don't let the energy burst out all at one time. Let that energy flow out of you in a controlled way, from the beginning of your presentation to the end. This will help you keep your audience engaged until you are done.

Now, back to the 35 business people at the workshop. Once the workshop participants understood my definition of FEAR and how to apply it to their advantage, I asked them if they would like to try to introduce themselves again. They all jumped at the opportunity. This time they stood, spoke energetically, and looked everyone in the eye while they introduced themselves. There was a completely different sense of confidence about them this time around. They also all acknowledged that they had felt fear the first time around, and that feeling of fear had prevented them from presenting themselves fully and well.

If you still feel you don't need to stand to introduce yourself, I have a question for you: If you were introducing a famous or important person to a group, would you stand to introduce him or her? Of course you would. You have respect for the person you're introducing. Why not treat yourself and your audience with the same esteem? If you want others to respect you, show respect for yourself and them.

One of the most important messages I want you to get from this book is: *it doesn't matter what anyone else does; it only matters what you do.* It's irrelevant whether anyone stood before you in a group setting. When it is your turn to introduce yourself, you need to stand, face everyone, and state your name clearly and energetically.

You are your own best marketing tool. How you present yourself says a great deal about you and your business. Since you often speak just as loudly with actions as you do with words, if you want others to perceive you as a confident person, act like a confident person.

A potential client base of hundreds

Here is another instance in which FEAR played a part. I was speaking at an event where the attendees represented 330 businesses from around the world. I asked the participants if they were familiar with the term "elevator speech" (this is when you have 30 seconds to introduce yourself and tell someone what you and your company can do). Everyone nodded their heads agreeing they knew what it was. I then asked, "Would anyone here like to give theirs?"

You could hear an audible chuckle run through the room but not one person stood up to speak. Not one person took advantage of the opportunity to present themselves or their company. Although all of the attendees had just been handed the opportunity to directly connect with 329 potential clients from around the world, fear had struck every one of them. How much would these businesses have paid a marketing firm to positively promote their companies to 329 potential clients all at one time? How amazing would it have been to have everyone walking out of the seminar remembering your name? Now that's the ultimate networking!

I have spoken to a large number of networking groups. I always arrive early because I want to watch how the participants greet each other. It amazes me how many people go to a networking function and never meet anyone new. Perhaps they are fearful of introducing themselves to new people. If they expect to succeed in business and life, however, they need to get over it.

When in doubt, listen

The fact of the matter is, we will all find ourselves in predicaments where we will need to face our fear. Here's a personal one of mine: a longtime friend had been playing with his grandchildren one evening when he fell down and hit his head on the floor. As a precautionary measure, his daughter took him to the local hospital, where the physician ordered an MRI scan of his head. Shockingly, the scan revealed six brain tumors, and the doctors gave Rudy six weeks to live.

At the beginning of this section I mentioned the fear of visiting a terminally ill friend. When contemplating this visit, I feared that I wouldn't know what to say to my friend Rudy. But knowing that there might only be a small window of opportunity to spend time with him, I didn't want to let that opportunity pass me by.

The first time I went to visit Rudy, he gave me an "out" after visiting with him for 15 minutes by saying, "It was nice of you to stop by." I said, "What are you doing, kicking me out?" He said he saw how uncomfortable most people were who came to visit him and he always wanted to give them an opportunity to leave. I told him that I was planning on having a couple of beers with him, that I hadn't even had my first one yet, and that frankly, the service around here was terrible. With that we both had a good laugh, and a moment later his wife appeared with a giant smile on her face and a beer in her hand.

Over the next six weeks I visited Rudy as often as I could. We talked about his favorite Christmas memories, his first car, his children, his grandchildren, his first bike, his first apartment, his wedding day, and about a large golfing trophy that I saw on his mantle. On closer inspection I had noticed that it was a memorial trophy that had been named after him. I asked him how many times he had won this trophy that had been named for him? He said he had never won it. I said, "Let me get this straight – your club has named a memorial trophy after you and you've never won it?" Our belly laughs lasted at least five minutes!

Here's the tip: when you are fearful of what to say in a situation like this, don't say much – listen instead. Resist the temptation to walk in and blurt out, "How are you doing?" I did that once (I was 14) to one of my father's friends who was terminally ill. He turned to me and said, "I'm dying, Donny, how should I be doing?" I felt like a cold knife had pierced my chest. Please learn from my mistake. Don't open the conversation with a thoughtless question or comment that can backfire on you.

What you can say is, "You are very important to me. I want to spend some time with you if you're up to it." Then ask him/her something that might be relevant or meaningful: his favorite holiday memory, first car, how he remembers a piece of history that you share, or an accomplishment he is most proud of, for example. As he goes back in time to chat about special memories, the conversation will unfold. You need only to continue to ask questions that interest you, based on what he has just talked about. (The skill of listening and asking good questions is covered in greater detail in a later section of this handbook titled: "Zip your Lips and Listen." Learning to do it well will come in handy for you in so many business and personal situations.)

The personal benefit I gained from our visits was that after Rudy passed, I had no regrets. I spent time with him when he needed me most, and we bonded in a very meaningful way. It turned out that overcoming my private fear and listening to my dying friend was an act of love I was able to give him at the end of his journey.

Facing public fear

Rudy's funeral was held at a church where he had been a member for over 45 years. There were over 450 people in attendance, and when the priest came up to give his eulogy, I heard him say, "I heard that Rudy was a quiet man." I was shocked and disappointed. This man was going to eulogize my friend, but he obviously didn't know him. My wife leaned over in the pew and said, "What are you going to do about that?"

Fear literally gripped me at that moment. I could practically taste it. There were hundreds of people present and I had not been asked to speak; but I could not allow my dear friend to be eulogized by a priest who was a stranger to him. I felt someone who knew Rudy needed to say something, so I stood up and started to walk towards the front of the church along the side aisle. When I got to the front of the church I stopped and looked up at the priest standing behind the pulpit. Since I stand seven feet tall, I thought he would surely see and acknowledge me, but he didn't.

At that moment, my FEAR energized me. With my heart beating out of my chest, I walked right up to the priest while he was still talking. I told him that I had to say something about my friend Rudy. He looked away for a moment, and when he turned back, I simply said, "Please," with all the emotion I was feeling. After that, he backed away from the pulpit.

To tell you the truth I can't remember everything that I said that day. I do remember that I wanted his friends to know how much he appreciated the golf trophy being named after him. I wanted them to know what a good laugh we had had about that. And I wanted his grandchildren to know how much he was going to miss their sporting events and that he had said to me, "Perhaps now I will be able to see them all." When I was finished, the priest returned to the pulpit and simply said, "Amen."

Facing these fears was not an earth-shattering achievement, but it made a big difference in my life and in the memorial experiences of Rudy's family and friends. There will be numerous opportunities in your lifetime to say something that is in your heart. Don't allow fear to rob you of the opportunity to say it, because you may regret it for the rest of your life. Take your fear and put it to good use.

APPLY THIS IN YOUR LIFE:
Watch how others introduce themselves. Notice the difference between someone who stands and one who does it sitting down. The next time you have the opportunity to introduce yourself, and you will find plenty of chances to do so, stand tall and use your FEAR to speak with energy and confidence. It will set you apart from the crowd in a very positive way. In fact, I have actually landed speaking engagements simply by introducing myself in such a fashion. Don't let fear paralyze you. Understand that we all feel it - it is how you deal with it that counts.

Track when you practiced these techniques and how it benefitted you.

_____

_____

_____

_____

_____

_____

_____

_____

_____

_____

"Send out a cheerful, positive greeting, and most of the time
you will get back a cheerful, positive greeting.
It's also true that if you send out a negative greeting,
you will, in most cases, get back a negative greeting."

~ *Zig Ziglar*

Great Greetings And Goodbyes

Every relationship starts with a hello. Who gave you your best hello today? Take a moment and think about it. Chances are you can give me a name. I find it interesting that within a few seconds people of all ages can tell me who gave them their best hello, or whether anyone has said hello to them at all.

One man responded to the question with, "My dog." Think about that. Dogs give great hellos. They are completely focused on you. They act like they can't wait to see you, and they meet you at the door.

A lot of the participants in my lectures will answer that I gave them their best hello. But that's not surprising, since I am consciously trying to be their best hello and I already know that people will remember me if I do.

My question to you is this: if I asked everyone you came in contact with over the last 24 hours, "Who gave you your best hello," would any of them say it was you? If you think they would, kudos to you. If you aren't sure, now's your opportunity to learn to be that person.

In some of my lectures I speak for over 90 minutes on how to say hello to someone. I spend that much time on the subject because it is that important. You have roughly five seconds to make a great first impression, and I want to ensure that you do. Understanding the fact that people remember who gave them their best hello will give you a huge advantage over others.

We think we are good at networking and building relationships, yet we are often unaware of the impression (or lack of impression!) we leave with a new person in those first five seconds. It is so important to make a connection immediately. Rather than walking through life on autopilot, giving out thousands of automatic, apathetic hellos, be aware that you are constantly being perceived. Leave a lasting positive impression.

I was working with an introverted young man we will call Sam, who was preparing to go away to college. To help Sam get over his fear of greeting people and to help him understand the importance of giving a great hello, I took him to the local shopping mall early one Saturday morning. There were plenty of mall walkers present and I told Sam "I just want you to greet three different people." It just so happened that three older gentlemen were approaching us, one behind the other and evenly spaced apart. As the first man passed, Sam said, "Good morning," but the gentleman never broke stride, didn't look at us and just kept walking. The same thing happened with the second and third gentleman.

After watching that scenario I told Sam, "Let me show you how this is done." I took him over to the food court, which was not yet open for business. There was a man behind one of the counters; bent down with his back to us, removing needed items from a cabinet along the back wall. As I walked by I raised an open hand towards him and with a loud voice said, "hello!" The man turned his head around, saw me smiling and looking him in his eyes. He saw my hand opened towards him and he felt the energy that I was consciously aiming at him. He responded by standing up, turning completely around to face me and greeting me with his energy and a smile. "That is what I am talking about Sam," I said. "You need to give something of yourself, whether it's energy, enthusiasm or effort. Don't be afraid to connect."

Sam was giving people the best hello he could at the time, but he needed to understand that his hellos were not getting good results. He needed to practice, practice, practice; and he did. Sam has since graduated from college, and he never fails to tell me how much that day at the mall changed his life forever.

I want you to see that you matter. When I ask a high school student at two o'clock in the afternoon, "Who gave you your best hello today?" and he/she honestly tells me that nobody has said hello to them that day, it proves to me that the other students, teachers and faculty don't realize how much they matter.

How many people could *you* have said hello to today? We are given 86,400 seconds a day. I encourage you to invest 60 seconds to give 60 people the second it takes to greet them with enthusiasm, energy, sincerity and purpose. In the end it will benefit *you*.

Who are you saving it for?

I often ask people that I am meeting for the first time, "Is that your best hello?" When they say, "No it wasn't," I ask them, "Who are you saving it for?" You have no idea who you may meet today who could change your life forever. For those of you who are married, could you have predicted that you would fall in love and make a permanent commitment before you met your spouse? What a difference meeting one person can make in our lives.

Since you do not know whom you will meet today, it's time to start consciously giving your best hellos. As you do this, pay particular attention to how the person reacts. Did you get their attention, eye contact, a smile and a response? That is how you will know if you've given a great hello.

Observe the people around you at home, at work, and in the community, and identify those who could use a cheerful hello. The person's body language or expression may be a clue as to their current state. You will not need to look far to find someone who could use a great greeting. In your workplace, a positive and memorable greeting can actually improve your work life and your career opportunities, so be attentive to how you greet everyone you see in that environment.

When you give your best hello, be sincere, authentic and focused on the person you are greeting. Invest your energy in the effort (more on this in "Increase Your Energy Level") and look the person in the eyes. Recognize your powerful ability to influence everyone around you in a positive way. Interestingly, when you witness the positive impact this has on people, it will strengthen your own self-confidence and encourage you to continue your efforts.

Cost versus benefit

What is the cost associated with giving a great hello? A lot of people in my sessions have said it doesn't cost anything, but there is a cost. If there were no cost, everyone would be doing it. The cost is emotional and physical: it includes adopting a permanent attitude of being truly interested in others, and investing energy in your interpersonal interactions every time. It is also a willingness to give away a part of your psyche and your personal store of energy to everyone you meet.

Fortunately, the cost of offering your best hello is far exceeded by the direct benefits. When you see how people respond to you and observe how your energy impacts those you greet, it strengthens your own self worth and may increase the energy and goodwill you receive in return. For each investment of energy and attitude, you may get back more than you put in, since one uplifting interaction may ripple out and connect you to others over time.

Your phone voice matters, too
When you answer your home or cell phone, do you invest conscious energy? Do you sound sincere? Did you know that people can 'hear' facial expressions, so they will know whether or not you are smiling as you speak? Whether you are face-to-face with a person or on the telephone, the same principles apply.

Your voicemail greeting can have an even more critical impact. This recorded projection of your personality and attitude creates a listener's perception of you. If listened to repeatedly (as family, friends, colleagues and customers will), it can make those perceptions more permanent. What people hear says a great deal about you. Put some thought into what you want your listeners to hear, and how you want to sound to them, then script and record your work and home phone messages to create that perception.

Great goodbyes
Just as important as a great hello is an impactful goodbye. It may even be more important because this is the last impression people will have of that experience with you.

When you are shaking hands at the end of a professional interaction, be sure to look the person in the eyes. *When your hand is in someone else's hand, your eyes must be on their eyes, period.* Don't look around to see who else you want to connect with, or to look at the clock. Also, when the person you are saying goodbye to turns to leave, make sure you are the last one with eye contact. This way, if they turn around one last time, they will still see you looking at them. This may seem like an insignificant detail, but it could impact how impressed the person is with your attention to them.

The same level of effort can help you build strong, lasting personal relationships as well. For example, when guests are leaving your home, do you get up out of your chair to say goodbye to them? Do you walk them to the door, or even out the door? Have you ever taken it even further and walked them to their car? Trust me, people will remember how far you escort them. Try walking your guests all the way to their car and then watching and waving as they drive away.

My best goodbye is part of my personal statement. I actually never say 'goodbye' to anyone. My ending comment is always "good morning." You will find I end all personal conversations and emails this way. My purpose is not only to be different, but also to convey to everyone the promise of a whole new day.

APPLY THIS IN YOUR LIFE:
Consciously decide to give your best hello to at least one person tomorrow. Be sincere, bring energy and maintain eye contact. Greet this person as you would like to be greeted. Since folks tend to remember who gave them their best hello, be his or her best hello for the day. At the end of your conversation, also offer a great goodbye. Make sure the person knows you enjoyed seeing them. Start using great greetings and goodbyes and watch how differently people react to you.

Track when you practiced these techniques and how it benefitted you.

_____

_____

_____

_____

_____

_____

_____

_____

_____

_____

"How your world reacts to you is a direct reflection
of how you are reacting to your world."

~ Donald Wayne McLeod

Have You Looked In The Mirror Lately?

I wear my 'coaching hat' every day, so I often end up coaching friends in
their personal relationships. One day I was listening to a friend of mine
end a phone conversation. He never said goodbye to the person he was
talking to; he simply hung up. When I asked him why he ended the
conversation so abruptly, he said that the person he was talking to was
being abrupt with him. I commented that it might be because of how he
sounded.

It just so happened that during the day I heard several more phone
conversations between my friend and that same person. Each
conversation seemed to frustrate my friend, and I could feel the tension
in the air. I asked him if he would perform an experiment for me. I asked
if he would answer the phone with a great hello the next time that person
called. I told him to change the tone in his voice, sound energetic and to
offer a great goodbye as well. To my delight, he did. When I asked him
what the response was, he told me the person sounded completely
different and agreeable. When they spoke again, the conversation I heard
was relaxed and stress-free.

I tell that story to illustrate the fact that how others react to us is a direct
reflection of how we are reacting and behaving with them. For example,
when was the last time someone truly encouraged you (and I don't mean
someone saying "nice shirt")? If you're having trouble recalling when
someone was compassionate or supportive with you, perhaps it's because
you are not a supportive, encouraging person yourself.

If you aren't getting encouragement from those around you, what else
might you be doing without because of your own reactions and behavior?
This is a sobering thought. If you're walking down the street and no one
is saying hello to you, what does that tell you? If you walk into a store
that you have frequented more than five times and no one knows your

name, what does that say about you? If you walk into work and people don't make much effort to greet you or seek you out, what does this say about your professional behaviors? If people don't take the time to truly listen to you, what message should you get about how you treat them? Are you listening to what the world is telling you... about you? If you want the world around you to change, you need to understand that the change begins with you.

The same holds true at networking events. A lot of people have told me that they haven't gained any benefit from going to networking functions. They complain that they haven't landed a job or increased their business. But they fall silent when I ask them, "Who is the last person you helped land a job, and to whom have you referred business in this group?" They don't comprehend the fact that others haven't helped them because they haven't helped others.

If you're waiting for someone to come up and give you their full attention, you may be waiting a long time. If you want them to show interest in your business or your elevator speech, it won't happen just because you're in the room. But, here's the good news: since so few people make the effort to engage with others dynamically and meaningfully, it doesn't take much to make yourself stand out from the crowd.

Understand that you have a great deal of influence on how people perceive and respond to you. Don't wait for others to change – *you* must be the change. Start bringing energy into your networking, and spread it around. Start greeting people with meaningful hellos. Once you behave and react positively to the people in your world, they will do the same for you.

APPLY THIS IN YOUR LIFE:
It is impossible to be a positive, energetic and encouraging person without it bouncing back to you. Start stepping out with a smile, give of yourself, show an interest in those around you and extend your influence in a positive way, and watch how your world reacts to you.

Track when you practiced these techniques and how it benefitted you.

_____

_____

_____

_____

_____

_____

_____

_____

_____

_____

_____

_____

_____

_____

_____

_____

_____

_____

_____

> "Passion is energy.
> Feel the power that comes from
> focusing on what excites you."
>
> ~ *Oprah Winfrey*

Increase Your Energy Level

Are people *passing on* your name or simply *passing* on your name? A subtle difference in how it is said but a world of difference as to how it impacts your life. Wouldn't it be great if you had five people actively promoting and passing on your name on a daily basis? Imagine just five people speaking positively about you to their friends, family, co-workers, neighbors, chambers, clubs and social networks. Do you think that would help your business grow, help you land the job of your dreams, or help you get your marketing message out? Beyond a doubt!

I truly believe that you can accomplish astounding things in this life if you can inspire others to help you. I said *inspire* others, rather than convince others, for a reason. 'Convince' implies getting them to help you meet your goals, while 'inspire' implies a willingness to give of their own free will for us, regardless of the goal. But how do you inspire others to want to help you?

First of all, be passionate about things that are important to you. People who are truly passionate add a natural energy to whatever they do. If you are not excited about what you are doing, why should anyone else be excited about helping you do it? I often ask people what their motivation is for doing what they do. I didn't start my business because I'm passionate about making money. What I am passionate about is helping other people achieve their goals. This is the driving force in my life; I want to help others, especially young people, succeed in life and work. Because I am passionate I naturally bring energy to what I do, and people feel that energy.

Passion plus energy equals inspiration

I remember driving by a high school where I wanted to offer a presentation. I had corresponded several times via email with Trish (the person with the authority to bring me in to the school), to no avail. While driving by the high school on this particular day, I remember asking myself, "What's your motivation for speaking here?" The response was loud and clear in my head, "I want to help those kids achieve their goals in life." With that thought in my mind, I turned my car around and pulled into the parking lot. I was done e-mailing – I wanted a face-to-face meeting with the person in charge. I wasn't concerned about being rejected because it wasn't about me at that point. It didn't matter that walking in uninvited was uncomfortable for me. All that mattered was helping those kids.

Passionate, energized, and excited, I walked into the school. Arriving at the main office I asked if I could please speak to Trish. When Trish arrived at the office she looked at me and coldly said, "You have five minutes." I tried to explain that there was a lot more information than I could possibly share with her in five minutes. She reiterated, "You have five minutes." So, I made the most of those five minutes to explain my reason for wanting to speak to the students. I was passionate and energized, and Trish became totally engaged. In fact, she was so engaged in our conversation that after an hour and a half she stated, "We need you here."

My five minutes turned into an hour and a half because I was passionate about what I wanted to do for the students and animated in the way I spoke to her, and all of it was driven by the energy I invested in the conversation. As a result, I held Trish's attention long enough to inspire her.

You can inspire others to help you by sharing your passion and investing your energy. People respond to energy levels. They interpret the presence of energy as sincerity, and conversely perceive a lack of energy as insincerity. Had I presented my case with no energy during that meeting, I would have been given only five minutes and there would be no story.

Energy creates confidence, communicates attitude, and reveals character. It can put a spring in your step, a gleam in your eye, and a smile on your face. Human energy engages, persuades, influences and connects people. It can be given, received, and renewed on a daily basis. Energy is timeless and priceless, and yet it can be given freely. Energy is powerful and undeniable, and it is critical for building long-lasting interpersonal relationships. The energy (or lack of it) that you direct outward is received and interpreted by those around you, and is totally under your control. With all this in mind, it would be a waste of effort not to invest energy in everything you do.

Where does this personal energy come from? Have you ever watched a sporting event and seen the crowd go crazy, jump up and down, cheer themselves hoarse, and 'high-five' complete strangers? I think this is one reason people love going to sporting events; it affords them an opportunity to experience the exciting adrenaline rush that can result from the collective energy of a crowd, and it feels great. The question is, did the energy bursting out of all those people come from inside them or from an outside source?

I believe that potential energy is inside us all the time, lying dormant until triggered by outside people, forces or events. We can learn to tap into that energy; to build it up internally by focusing on things we are passionate or excited about and then using the energy that comes from those feelings. As we get better at it, we can sustain the energy for longer periods. I can feel energy in my body as I write this section because I'm passionate about this subject.

Developing this skill is a lot like getting into physical shape. Unless you are in great physical shape you could not drop and do a hundred push-ups. But you can start by trying to do one, then two, then five and ten. If you keep working at it, you can build up to doing a hundred. Use your energy to build excitement about connecting with other people. If you're not excited about meeting others, why should they feel excited about meeting you (see the section called Great Greetings and Goodbyes)? Make sure you are calling up energy not only when meeting someone for the first time, but every time you interact.

Energy is not only perceivable, it is marketable!™
Here is a case in point: when starting some lectures I walk around introducing myself to people who are seated in the room. After meeting at least three of them I ask the group, "If you were hiring just one person at your company, based on what you just saw, which of the people I just interacted with would you hire? In every case, the crowd picks the person who exhibited the most energy.

At other lectures I ask, "Who brought energy with them today?" Commonly no hands are raised or a few hands are lazily raised below shoulder level. I thank them for their honesty and then ask them if they feel energy in the room. They all agree that they feel energy in the room.

When I ask where they feel it's coming from, they reply that it's coming from me. After facilitating a typical two-hour session I am wringing wet from the energy pouring out of my body. I also feel my energy bounce back to me through my audience's attention and participation.

I tell them they feel the energy coming from me because I understand the value and benefits of investing energy in all I do. I also continually practice to build my energy so that I can give it to my audiences. I want to inspire others to help me, so I energize them. Who in your life is energizing you? Probably someone you care about deeply and want to help. More importantly, who is receiving your energy?

I conduct informal exercises to help groups assess the energy levels coming from one another. I have participants get up and speak in front of the group. The speakers do not know ahead of time that they are going to be judged, and the listeners don't know they will be the judges. Once they're done speaking, I ask the class to assess the speakers' energy levels. My scale is my arm: arm down at my side represents zero; my arm raised straight out at shoulder level is a "five;" and my arm straight up over my head is a 10, the maximum. While slowly raising my arm from the zero position, I tell the class to raise their hand when my arm reaches the point that represents each speaker's energy level. In most instances all the hands are raised before my arm is shoulder high (five on the scale). It continues to amaze me how many people speak with low energy, and how even their newly aware group peers can sense it during this exercise.

The TV show Deal or No Deal is a great example of how energy sells. No one would watch the show if the announcer and contestants spoke in quiet, monotone voices and if the theater audience was low key. If you are familiar with the show, you know the host moves the show along with dramatic flair and energy, contestants are animated and running around on the stage yelling out loud and agonizing over their decisions; and the audiences are encouraged to react loudly and often. Why? Because the producers and director know that maintaining a high energy level will keep millions of people glued to their TVs. Energy is a recognized marketing tool in this industry.

Bottom line: energy attracts others to you and your messages. If you want others to listen and be inspired, pour some energy into what you are saying.

APPLY THIS IN YOUR LIFE:
I want you to practice building up energy inside yourself. Whatever it is that makes you feel excited or passionate, tap into it. Maybe the first time, you just feel a little adrenaline rush that lasts a second or two. The next time, it may last longer, and eventually you'll be able to build up that high-energy feeling to last 30 seconds, several minutes, or even an hour.

Also, practice becoming consciously aware of your energy level at all times. Be excited about meeting others and watch how they respond to you. Don't just invest the energy to fill your seat – call up enough energy to fill the room. Inspire others to help you by putting good energy into your communication. You want people to not only see you, but feel you.

Track when you practiced these techniques and how it benefitted you.

_____

_____

_____

_____

_____

_____

_____

_____

_____

_____

_____

_____

"Jack Kennedy always told me, Hedy, get involved. That is the secret of life. Try everything. Join everything. Meet everybody.

~ Hedy Lamarr

Join In!

Too many of us are content to sit on the sidelines watching life pass us by. We complain about being lonely or bored, but we don't do anything to change our condition. In order to be truly alive and actively engaged in life, we must join in.

If you want to build interpersonal relationships with others, join in and be truly interested in what they are interested in. If friends ask you to come over to the house for a party, bring your whole self to that party – your energy, enthusiasm and full attention. Be excited! Don't go to be entertained but rather participate fully to help the host entertain. Take some of the information you've learned in this handbook and apply it. Be *interested* rather than *interesting*, and don't forget to ask questions and listen. If you see someone sitting alone, go over and speak with him or her.

Try to see the event through the eyes of the people who invited you. It is obviously important to them, or they wouldn't have wanted to include you. Make sure you conclude the event by expressing gratitude for the opportunity.

My brother, who has season tickets to the Ohio State University football games, has expressed his frustration to me in the past about people he invites to games who go but don't engage with the event. "They don't care about the game at all," he says. "They act like they're doing me a favor coming to the game, and just sit there."

When he invites me to a game I am 'all about them Buckeyes.' One of my brother's favorite parts of the game is when the Ohio State Marching Band takes the field during pregame festivities. The drum major must bend over backwards until his hat touches the turf, at which point the band can advance onto the field. I enjoy it because my brother enjoys it.

I am interested because he is interested. I want to be invited back, so I join in the experience with my host, whether it's my brother, a friend, or a client.

Change it up

To increase your interpersonal opportunities, go places where you can meet new people and vary the places you visit. If possible, sit in a different seat every time you go to a regular event so that you can talk to different people. Another great opportunity to build personal relationships is at children's activities and sporting events. If you want a sure-fire way to strengthen friendships, support your friends' kids.

Joining in also applies to conversations. When joining a conversation, stick with the current topic, be interested in what is being discussed, listen actively and ask relevant questions. Avoid being the competitive person who has to outdo another person's story or force a change of topic.

I was at a local restaurant one day, seated by a table of six elderly ladies having lunch together. I overheard one of the ladies sharing a rather shocking story from her childhood. Her little brother had accidentally punctured her lung by throwing a dart that penetrated her back.

Wow, I thought. If I were a member of that group I would ask her more detailed questions about that experience. Unfortunately, as soon as she stopped speaking her friend piped up with, "When I was a kid...." I thought to myself, now that is human nature. People feel they have to tell a bigger and better story. Mistake! A tremendous opportunity just passed to learn more about a friend. Instead, someone else was craving the spotlight.

APPLY THIS IN YOUR LIFE:
Your mission is to join in. The next time you are invited somewhere, go with the intention of participating fully. While you are there, be involved. Join in the conversation and stay on topic. Understand why the event is important to the person and reinforce their excitement. Make it a point to learn something new about the people you are with.

Track when you practiced these techniques and how it benefitted you.

_____

_____

_____

_____

_____

_____

_____

_____

_____

_____

_____

_____

_____

_____

_____

_____

_____

_____

_____

_____

"It is one of the beautiful compensations of life, that no man can sincerely help another without helping himself."

~ Ralph Waldo Emerson

Kudos For All

One day, I was sitting around my dining room table with the in-law side of my family (if you don't know the difference between in-laws and outlaws... outlaws are wanted — just kidding!). I love and enjoy my in-laws immensely, and I work at my relationships with each of them individually.

Most of the family members present that particular day had just returned from witnessing my seven-year-old niece Katelyn Nicole's piano recital. This included my wife Karen and her Aunt June. June is 92, and had come in from California to stay with us for a couple of weeks. It takes a typical 92-year-old a bit more time and effort to get up, shower, and get ready to go anywhere. For this occasion, Aunt June spent four hours getting ready to watch Katelyn Nicole perform.

June and Karen left to see the performance nearby, while I stayed at home to finish preparing dinner for the family members who were coming to our house afterwards.

Ten minutes after the ladies left, Karen and June came walking back into the house. Karen said, "I'll bet you think we forgot something." It turned out that their timing had been perfect. They arrived just in time to see Katelyn Nicole perform her number. Our niece got up, dressed to the nines with her nails done and hair extensions on, and walked down the aisle. She passed the small crowd gathered for the recital, sat down at the piano and played da, da, da, da... da, da, da, da. That was it; eight notes. She then stood and took her bow.

Afterwards, when the family all gathered at our house for dinner, everyone around the table was congratulating Katelyn, and rightly so. She had faced her fear of playing in front of a crowd. Everyone was telling her how brave she was and how well she had played. This was appropriate, since it's very important to encourage children when they step up to the plate and take a swing. Whether they hit a home run or strike out isn't as important as the fact that they try.

However, I realized the irony of this unending praise as I looked down to the far end of the table at my father-in-law, Charlie. My niece was still receiving kudos for playing her eight notes, while Charlie, who had retired several years earlier from a public school system in which he had worked for 35 years without missing a day, had received no recognition at all from the school system or his colleagues. This got me thinking: who else at this table deserves kudos?

Why no elder praise?

Why is it so easy to congratulate children for simple tasks, but so difficult to praise adults for truly honorable or outstanding achievements? As children we were accustomed to older people validating us. Typically, parents praise a good report card or tell us that the picture we are drawing is beautiful, or the basket we score is worth screaming about. We need that as children and it encourages us to feel good about our abilities and ourselves.

But how many of us can remember telling our mothers, "Nice job on the dinner Mom, the pork was delicious," or telling our fathers, "The yard looks great!"? How many of us have thanked our parents for working hard to raise us well, teach us values, and financially support us until we are independent and able to care for ourselves? How meaningful a little sincere appreciation could be if sent in the opposite direction.

Why is it so hard to give kudos to our elders? When do the pats on the back and the "at-a-boys" stop coming? It may vary in families, but eventually it typically does. Ironically, we usually stop receiving validation from friends and family just when we need it the most. When we are thrown into the real world, and the proverbial you-know-what hits the fan, we often lose the praise that has helped us to that point. The question I pose is, why?

As adults we are expected to face the world head-on and to motivate ourselves to move forward in life. Life is so full of responsibilities that every one of us could use a personal secretary. There are daily, weekly and monthly duties. There are careers to be developed, investments to be considered, and plans to be made for the family's future. And, in many households, there are young people to raise and eventually, seniors to care for. Yet during these adult years, it seems the praise stops coming.

I have heard several theories behind this phenomenon. Some say it is because children are perceived as competition at a certain point and we do not want them to be more successful than we are. Others think that as they grow up, children become adversarial (especially as teens and young adults) so we want to humble them a bit to prepare them for the adult world. Others think it's jealousy; since we ourselves are not receiving kudos, why should we praise those around us?

I believe that it's easy to encourage children because we feel superior to them. We have no problem walking up and giving them a pat on the back for merely attempting to succeed. We have been there, done that. We have authority over them and so we feel confident in validating them. We also may believe that what we have to say will be meaningful to them.

The next evening Charlie, Karen, Aunt June, my mother-in-law Mary and I went to dinner. The three ladies were at one end of the table and Charlie sat directly across from me at the other end. While the ladies were chatting with each other, I leaned across to Charlie and shared with him what I had been thinking about the day before. I also sincerely thanked him for being a strong, quiet example to me of how people should conduct themselves. I congratulated him on his career achievements and let him know I appreciated him. My intention was to let him know that he was worth praising.

Charlie's response was one of quiet reserve and humility. He said he was just doing what was expected of him. And yet, I could see his eyes light up as he sat a little taller in his chair. I had simply given him a little long-overdue validation, and I knew my words meant something to him. Ironically, this realization also made me feel good inside. I also believe that my effort helped strengthen our relationship. I gave a little and received a lot, reinforcing the adage once again.

A friend later asked me if I ever complimented Aunt June for her ability to care for herself at the age of ninety-two. I missed that one at the time, but have contacted her since then to say that.

Everyone needs validation, regardless of age, sex, or station in life. It is amazing how we can positively impact ourselves and those around us if we simply look for things we can sincerely praise, compliment or verbally acknowledge about others. As you step up and give recognition to others, your own self-confidence grows, and this can have a snowball effect. The greater your self-confidence, the more willing you are to praise children, peers, colleagues, customers, bosses, and others you meet, and so it grows for everyone.

APPLY THIS IN YOUR LIFE:

Be different. At your next opportunity, step up and let someone know that you think well of them. In conversations, ask questions to discover something to admire, compliment or validate about them, and then tell them. If there is someone already in your life who could use a compliment, give him/her a meaningful one. People want to believe that they are valuable and appreciated, so you will be pleased at the response you get. The more you offer kudos, the easier it will become to change the responses around you.

Track when you practiced these techniques and how it benefitted you.

_____

_____

_____

_____

_____

_____

_____

_____

_____

_____

_____

_____

"I've always made a total effort, even when the odds
seemed entirely against me. I never quit trying;
I never felt that I didn't have a chance to win."

~ Arnold Palmer

Lottery Odds

Have you ever won the Super Lotto? I have a friend who did, and then
failed to cash in the winning ticket! Can you imagine anything more
exasperating? Have you ever thought about how your life would change
if you won a lottery? Do you think it would change the way you
approach each day? Do you think you might be more cordial to those you
see on a daily basis? Would you have a spring in your step or become
more aware of your ability to help others?

Here are some odds to think about. You have a 600 to one chance your
child will be considered a genius (that is, unless you talk to grandparents,
because every grandchild is one!). The odds of hitting that elusive hole-
in-one on a par three hole on a golf course are 5,000 to one (unless it's
me – I can hit 5,000 tee shots and never get it in the hole). Your chances
of being struck by lightning are 500,000 to one, which sounds pretty
good until you realize there are billions of us on the planet, so that means
a significant number of people are being struck by lightning). Your odds
of winning the Super Lotto are 20 million to one. No wonder few of us
know anyone who has won this lottery; the odds are pretty low. Now
imagine actually winning, and then failing to cash in the ticket!

There is another lottery that has even greater odds than the Super Lotto.
The conservative odds of winning are usually 200 million to one.
Imagine for a moment the prize for winning such a lottery. What would
you do with the winnings and do you think it would dramatically change
your life? You know it would.

For one thing, you would feel astoundingly lucky. Perhaps that alone
would put a spring in your step and have you giving everyone you meet a
better hello each day. It would most certainly affect your daily life from
that moment forward.

Well here is what you've won: on the day you were conceived, there were conservatively 200 million other sperm cells vying for the same prize – *life*! Any one of those cells would have created an entirely different person. You literally won a 200 million-to-one Super Lotto. This is a proven and undeniable fact. My question to you is, "Have you cashed in your ticket?" If you never realized you won, how could you? Could the friend who failed to cash in his/her winning ticket be you?

Too many of us are oblivious to the fact that we have already won the only lottery that really matters and are instead playing to win lesser prizes. *Hear this*: you represent over 200 million people who never got the chance to be on the planet. You have won more than money, and more than fame. You have won a chance to make a difference to all around you. You can accomplish anything in this life if you can inspire others to help you.

Are you really living your life to its full potential or are you too afraid to cash in your ticket? Realize that no matter how great the odds are that you face in life, they are nothing compared to the odds you already faced and beat! Congratulations!

You might now feel a certain amount of responsibility as the representative of 200,000,001 people. Don't let that paralyze you. If something is stopping you from doing the one thing you truly want to do with your life, stop waiting around to hit another lottery. Instead, appreciate the fact that you are a winner and start acting like one. You will notice a spring in your step, and so will everyone you come in contact with. Your winning attitude will make you stand out in a positive way.

APPLY THIS IN YOUR LIFE:
Now that you realize what a true miracle your life is and how fortunate you are to have been given this chance, seize your opportunities. Make a list of your life goals (a 'bucket list') and start researching what it would take to achieve them. Choose one goal and begin working toward it with the attitude of a winner. Take notes on your progress, and on how you are feeling about yourself as you progress.

Track when you practiced these techniques and how it benefitted you.

_____

_____

_____

_____

_____

_____

_____

_____

_____

_____

_____

_____

_____

_____

> "Go oft to the house of thy friend,
> for weeds choke the unused path."
>
> ~ *Ralph Waldo Emerson*

Maintain Your Relationships

If someone handed you a bunch of tomato seeds and you threw them in your dresser drawer, would you expect them to bear fruit? Of course not. Similarly, how many business cards have you been given that are tucked away and collecting dust somewhere? You need to think of each and every contact as a tomato seed, capable of bearing fruit if it is properly planted, nurtured and maintained.

In order to achieve success in this life, you are going to need the help of others. This handbook was written with the intention of helping you build meaningful, lasting relationships with others so that you can optimize your success. One of the most important parts of building your network is maintaining the relationships you already have. If you don't maintain your relationships you are simply compiling a list of strangers.

It is often the case that the person who can help you the most is already in your network – you just haven't built the meaningful relationship that would inspire them to help you. Dust off and revisit your contact lists, then start working on strengthening those relationships. If you can't do this with the people you already know, chances are you won't be able to do it with people you meet in the future.

For example, when was the last time you went through your contact list and simply dropped a 'hello email' to someone? The next time you have some down time think about doing it. You will be amazed at what a simple email such as, "Was thinking of you today, Judy. Please let me know how you are doing," will do. It could trigger a detailed response. Why? Because you may be the only one who is taking the time to touch base with Judy. Be different from everybody else and start employing the techniques you are learning in this handbook. If you want to build meaningful, lasting and productive relationships nurture the seeds you already have.

The best way to nurture relationships is to connect with people on a personal level with no strings attached. Sports are one easy topic of personal connection. Do you know if any of your contacts are NFL, NBA, NHL or MLB fans? You should know the teams they root for so you can drop them a line of encouragement throughout the season and share in their despair or revel in their joy, depending on how their teams perform. Think that would help grow your relationship? You bet (pun intended)!

You can also connect by knowing their birthdays and anniversaries, or when they receive special recognitions, and can congratulate them on these. You can wish the people in your network well on their preferred holidays – Christmas, New Year's Day, Hanukkah, Kwanzaa, Saint Patrick's Day, Easter, etc. These are simple but highly effective connection builders. Are you touching base with your contacts?

Make good use of social media
Media channels can also be a good source of information about some of your connections. It's a good idea, for example, to peruse local television or radio newscasts from time to time to see if any of your contacts or their family members are in the news. If so, send them a note. If you are a LinkedIn member, make sure that you have linked up with all your professional contacts by inviting them into your network. Then you can see daily updates from your contacts, you can endorse or recommend them, and you can post comments. Every genuine conversation or communication you participate in on social media channels (Facebook, Twitter and LinkedIn) can help grow your networks and relationships. Figure out how you can use your network to help others. Be the person who helps grow the relationship by asking how *you* can help *them* achieve their ultimate goals in life. If it's all about you, you are limiting your own possibilities. Helping others achieve their goals will ultimately help you achieve yours.

Another reason to maintain your network is the power of timing. You may have met people five years ago who are now in the position to help if you kept the relationships alive. You may meet people today who are the necessary catalyst to spur other contacts into action. I have experienced this myself; I met an individual who placed his stamp of approval on me, and this spurred three other contacts to hire me to present to their companies.

APPLY THIS IN YOUR LIFE:
Schedule time in your week to reach out to the people in your network. Find out what sports teams they follow and make a note of it. Acknowledge their birthdays, anniversaries and accomplishments. Ask them how they are doing. You will be amazed at their replies. Interact with as many of them as possible, in the most appropriate way for that person (face to face, phone, social media, personal letter, e.g.). If you want to inspire others to help you, be their inspiration.

Track when you practiced these techniques and how it benefitted you.

_____

_____

_____

_____

_____

_____

_____

_____

> "Remember that a person's name is to that person
> the sweetest and most important sound
> in any language."
>
> ~ *Dale Carnegie*

Names Matter!

Remembering a person's name is the key to any relationship. When you are meeting someone for the first time, it's important to concentrate so that you can *get, remember and use* that person's name. It's even more important that you listen to *how* the person introduces him/herself to you. The person is, in effect, telling you how they want to be addressed. A lot of people miss this cue.

If someone introduces himself as Matthew, do not take liberties with his name and call him Matt. He just told you his name was Matthew, so that is his preference. If a woman introduces herself as Mary Margaret Smith, do not call her Maggie. It's Mary Margaret, and Mary Margaret instantly heard what you called her. If you want to build genuine personal relationships, remember that the foundation of a successful relationship is using the person's name correctly.

Furthermore, getting and using the person's name immediately is more important at that moment than any other topic of conversation. People don't typically relate any critical information about their life within the first five minutes after meeting you, so you can always say, "I'm sorry, where did you say you work?" or, "Where did you say you live?" Most of us instinctively understand why it's much more embarrassing, and insulting, to ask, "What did you say your name was?"

In fact, it can be so awkward asking someone for his/her name again that you would rather not even go there. You would rather walk away from the conversation saying, "Nice meeting you," when it would be so much more impressive to be able to say, "Nice meeting you, Donald Wayne." Believe me, people know whether you remember their name or not. Talk about poor first impressions!

Get it right

Proper pronunciation is another important success factor. Taking the time to learn how the person pronounces his/her name is critical. You would notice even a slight difference in the way your own name is pronounced. Believe me, *Mikala* will hear the difference if her name is pronounced '*Makala*,' and so will anyone else listening. It amazes me how many people don't realize that mispronouncing someone's name can damage the potential relationship with that person. How can you expect to build a relationship of trust with someone when you clearly don't care enough to learn how to say his/her name properly? Even worse, every time you say the name incorrectly, you reinforce that very notion.

Remember, how you are perceived is your reality. I can tell if someone is making the effort to remember my name as I meet him/her. (I will share a story about this in the section titled "Sincerity.") If a person feels that you forgot his/her name, you will be perceived as uncaring. People love the sound of their name, and I am no exception.

I'm so bad at remembering names…

If you appreciate the value of remembering names, but believe you are terrible at remembering them, my advice to you is… stop reinforcing that negative thinking. All you are doing is giving yourself an excuse. Rather than saying you're terrible with names, start reinforcing positive behavior from this moment forward. Start telling yourself how important names are and that you will *get, remember and use* people's names in the future.

People often ask me what tricks I use to remember names. I often write names and file them so that I can easily look them up later. After meeting people, I write down their name and jot down something that will help me remember them (e.g., green glasses, great smile, tall, energetic.) I also write down the names of spouses, kids and pets. However, the main reason I can remember people's names is because I understand how important their name is to *them*.

We have all been there

You see someone coming up to you and you can't remember his/her name to save your life. How uncomfortable is that? Wouldn't it be nice to be able to pull up their name in your mental contact list and greet them by name? With practice, you will remember names, and it will benefit you significantly.

Conversely, people you are approaching will appreciate your effort to make it easy for them. If I walk up to someone who I think might not remember my name, I will call him/her by name, state mine, and mention how they might know me. It relieves any anxiety they might feel and sets you up as a considerate person. Now, do I expect you to remember the names of all the people you meet? Absolutely not, but I do expect you to remember their names while they're still in the room with you.

I once walked into an exclusive men's clothing store to buy a suit. As I walked in, there were four male employees, all of whom were looking at me. I was the only customer in the store, and I said in a loud voice, "My name is Donald Wayne McLeod and I am here to buy a suit. Who's selling it to me?"

I then started over to the side of the store that had my sizes. One of the men broke away from the group, came over and shook my hand, and told me his name was Mark. "Donald Wayne McLeod," I repeated, "nice to meet you, Mark." "Nice meeting you," Mark replied. "What is my name?" I asked. Mark just shook his head and said he couldn't remember. I looked back at the other three employees and asked, "Do any of you remember my name?"

One of the men replied, "You're Donald Wayne McLeod and you are here to buy a suit." I waved him over saying, "And you're the one who is selling it to me." Mark was mumbling, "You're right; I wasn't listening," as he walked away. I wanted to buy a suit, but I wanted to buy it from someone who was interested in me. I could have gone to any men's suit store, but what I wanted was service and attention to detail. I wanted to buy from someone who saw me as a person.

The manager of the store, who observed the whole event, came up to me later and said, "You know, Donald Wayne, Mark will never forget that lesson." I agreed and explained that what I did was deliberate. I put Mark through the quizzing not to hurt him, but to wake him up to the importance of personally connecting with his customers.

When you are eating at a restaurant, start making it a regular practice to get, remember and use your server's name. It will benefit you greatly. How nice it is when you need service and you can call that person by name as they walk by. Furthermore, you are highly likely to benefit from enhanced service from the person whose name you remember.

I *get, remember and use* people's names as often as possible. And, because I believe that a person's name is the key to his/her friendship, I will go one step further to stand out from the rest. When I get someone's name (let's say, Brian), I will then ask what his/her middle name is.

Most people use their middle initials in their official signatures and for their resumes. Middle names are usually printed out for all to see on birth certificates, diplomas, marriage licenses and wedding invitations. If it is an important document, it usually includes middle names. For these reasons, they could be considered names with added esteem.

When Brian tells me his middle name, I will comment on the name, "Brian Thomas, now that's a strong name. How nice to have a great name, I am sure you are proud of it." I will also ask if it's a family name and if there is a history behind it. It's amazing how easily a conversation can start from these questions. This is because I am showing a sincere interest. I will ask Brian if he will allow me to call him Brian Thomas. Nine out of ten times, the person will tell you to go right ahead, and you will often see delight in his/her eyes. An individual's full name is the sweetest sound in the world to him/her. The name was given for a special reason.

You might be thinking that the only time you heard your first and middle name together was when you were in trouble as a kid. But you also know that those who call you by your first and middle name love you. If you are going to afford me the luxury of calling you by a name that is used by those who love you, why wouldn't I? Your full name carries an association of closeness and caring. Can you see how using a person's first and middle name can help create or strengthen a relationship?

When a person gives you permission to use his/her middle name, use it. Use it every time you call, write, email or greet them. Believe me, he/she will notice. At first, it may feel a little weird using someone's middle name since it doesn't sound natural to you. But remember it *does* sound natural to the person who owns the name. I want you to think of your middle name. Is there history or a story attached to your name? Do you use your middle name or its initial in your signature or email? Does it sound funny to you to be called by your first and middle name or does it flow? Would you mind someone using your middle name? Can you hear someone calling you by it in your head?

When saying someone's middle name, treat it with all due respect and dignity. No matter what the person tells you their middle name is, say it clearly and as if it is the sweetest sound on earth. Remember it is their name and as such, it is important to them. Whether it's Roger or Rumpelstiltskin, repeat it carefully. There are a lot of things you can overcome when building a relationship, but making fun of someone's name is not one of them.

I have been calling people by their first and middle name for a long time because I see how people react to it. For example, there was an 85-year old woman living in a gated community in California. She lived across the street from my aunt. Here name was Ruthie. I asked her for her middle name and she told me it was Ann. I asked her if I could call her Ruth Ann and she said yes. For the next two weeks every time I saw her I called her Ruth Ann. The funny thing was, months after my wife and I flew home, my aunt called to tell us that Ruthie was now Ruth Ann to everyone in the community! At 85 years of age, she had reclaimed the name she was so fond of, and she was known as Ruth Ann until the day she died.

Occasionally you will run into a person who does not like having their middle name used. If a person tells you they don't like their middle name or that they prefer you not use it, then don't. Respect their wishes. There is no reason to start a problem right at the beginning of a relationship. I promise that these people are few and far between.

Did you know that in a lot of foreign countries it is common practice to use middle names? In fact I have spoken to people from other countries who found it odd that Americans don't honor people by calling them by their first and middle names. You may want to start by using your family members' middle names until you get the hang of it. It might sound funny to you at first, but watch how fast that middle name blends right in. Katelyn Nicole (our niece) is like music to our ears now!

Joann C. Jones once told me this story:
"During my second year of nursing school our professor gave us a quiz. I breezed through the questions until I read the last one: 'What is the first name of the woman who cleans the school?' Surely this was a joke. I had seen the cleaning woman several times, but how would I know her name? I handed in my paper, leaving the last question blank. Before the class ended, one student asked if the last question would count toward

our grade. "Absolutely," the professor said. "In your careers you will meet many people. All are significant. They deserve to be acknowledged, even if all you do is smile and say hello." I've never forgotten that lesson. I also learned that her name was Dorothy.

APPLY THIS IN YOUR LIFE:
Next time you meet someone, concentrate on his/her name and commit it to memory. Write it down if you have to, and use it often during your conversation. Make sure you are pronouncing it properly and can spell it for future correspondence (don't assume you know how to spell Carol/Karol/Karell/Carole, for example). Do not take liberties with someone's name; say it just as they do.

Try getting and using the person's middle name (or try this with a relative) and watch how the person responds to it. I actually answer to 'Donald Wayne.' You may not be able to remember every person's name that you meet, but at least remember it while you are in the room with him/her. With practice and effort, *getting, remembering and using* names will become easier and will help you to stand out as a caring, respectful person.

Track when you practiced these techniques and how it benefitted you.

_____

_____

_____

_____

_____

_____

_____

_____

_____

"We are what we repeatedly do.
Excellence, then, is not an act, but a habit."

~ Artistotle

Orchestrate!

People often hear me say, "Remember to bring the orchestra." Translation: combine and utilize as many of the interpersonal skills in this handbook as possible, so that you are optimizing the potential of being perceived positively. The ability to blend and coordinate all these skills into a flawless personal presentation is a skill in itself, and one that I rarely see.

If you've ever had the pleasure of hearing a professional orchestra I'm sure you will agree it is spectacular. The conductor has a wide variety of professionally trained individual musicians, who can create a huge menu of sounds, tempos and volumes. The conductor directs and blends all the different components of the orchestra, from bombastic cymbals and tympani down to the ping of a single triangle or bell, to create a masterpiece. If you have ever studied conductors in action you've noticed how hard they need to concentrate. They are concentrating on every detail in order to make the presentation perfect, and it shows.

As with conducting an orchestra, successful networking is achieved through concentration, coordination and practice. First, we must learn the interpersonal skills required, and then practice them until they become flawless. Then, during networking opportunities, when we 'conduct' these combined skills with energy, style and grace, we help assure a positive perception.

The components we orchestrate for networking are the people skills that are at our disposal. People respond to how we talk, walk, dress and interact with others. We have components such as greetings, handshakes, eye contact, energy levels, listening skills, manners, goodbyes and body language that we can apply to effect a positive perception, if we coordinate and perform them well.

Are you an accomplished conductor? Are your interpersonal and communication skills polished and ready to go?

Not enough orchestras out there

The problem is, a lot of individuals are giving presentations that sound less like a professional orchestra and more like a grade school concert band. They are going through the motions, but the music is almost unrecognizable.

We have no idea who we will meet today who will change our lives forever. Everyone we meet is listening both consciously and unconsciously to our inner orchestra. What kind of music are others hearing coming from you? Do you sound sincere, gracious, positive, energetic and optimistic, or do you sound negative, insincere, uninterested, bored or self-absorbed?

The weak link

To achieve the best interactions, all the communication skills mentioned in this handbook need to be performed to the best of your ability. This is important because unfortunately, people usually remember a person's weakest performance area the most, so a weak skill could negatively affect how you are perceived.

Imagine you are listening to an orchestra. In a moment of absolute silence in the music, a musician drops the triangle. Now, what one thing do you think you will remember from that experience? How often do you think you will share that story with others?

You might have a great smile, fresh breath, high energy and a terrific handshake. You may be well-dressed, use terrific eye contact and converse smoothly. However, you meet someone and don't use her name, or worse yet, you call her by the wrong name. How is she likely to remember you?

Any one of the interpersonal communication skills mentioned could be your weak link. And there are others, such as manners, listening skills, verbal and writing skills, personal hygiene, patience, and more. Whenever you are networking, you are presenting a marvelous product – *you*. You will want the 'whole package' to present well and positively.

APPLY THIS IN YOUR LIFE:
Become more aware of how people around you do or don't 'bring the orchestra' by coordinating and performing at their personal best. Choose one person to observe, and evaluate his/her overall performance. What skills does he/she possess that you would consider positive, and what skills would you consider to be negative or detracting? Was there one particular weakness that you remember about them? Use what you learn to adjust your own personal orchestra, and continue to learn, apply and practice the useful skills in this handbook to achieve your 'personal best.'

Track when you practiced these techniques and how it benefitted you.

_____

_____

_____

_____

_____

_____

_____

_____

_____

_____

_____

_____

_____

_____

_____

_____

_____

_____

_____

> "People believe I am what they see me as,
> rather than what they do not see."
>
> ~ *Neale Donald Walsch*

Perception Is Your Reality

Every day the people we come in contact with perceive us on a multitude of levels. They observe our appearance, posture, speech, manners, eye contact, and so on. They may never even speak to us and yet they perceive us as confident, friendly, interesting or, unfortunately, perhaps as insecure, hostile or even boring. It's important to realize that our reality is not formed by how we perceive ourselves, but rather it is based on how *others perceive us*.

The following interaction actually took place during an evening class I was teaching to twelve adults. I asked one man in the group to tell us something about himself. He stated, "I am a very romantic person." His wife, who happened to be sitting right next to him looked over at him and matter-of-factly stated, "No you're not!" Unaltered by her response he looked directly at me and confidently stated again, "No really, I am a very romantic person." His wife then looked directly at me and emphatically said, "No, he's not!"

Because of the wife's response, I tested him by asking, "What's your wife's middle name?" He looked at me like a deer in headlights, unable to answer (I can't make this stuff up). I then very slowly asked him, "When is her birthday?" He just sat there unresponsive and unable to answer the question. In his own mind he still considered himself a very romantic person, but his reality, and his wife's, were quite different.

I addressed the husband directly; "The only person who can truly say you are a romantic person is sitting right next to you... are you listening?" It didn't matter what he thought about himself in this area of his life; what mattered was his wife's perception of him, since she was the recipient of his romantic attention (or lack of it).

Listen!

Here is another example. During PERCEPTIONOLOGY® sessions, I have individuals get up and address the rest of the attendees. After each speaker finishes presenting, I ask him/her, "Who was your best listener?" Interestingly, people can generally discern who is listening and who is not, so most of the time, the speaker can readily tell me who their best listener was.

A word to the wise: they can also tell me who their *worst* listener was, so you may prefer to be remembered as a great listener! During one such exercise the speaker named "Tom" as her worst listener. Well, Tom jumped out of his seat and started to tell us all that he could tell us everything that the speaker said, verbatim. He was passionate and seemed truly troubled by the fact he was singled out as the worst listener.

My response to Tom was that it didn't matter if he could tell us everything verbatim, it only mattered that he was perceived to be a poor listener. If the president of his company had been speaking, and had assessed him as not listening, that would become Tom's reality. He might then be subjected to any and all consequences that could result from that perception, such as being perceived as an uninterested or disengaged employee, being blacklisted, or being passed over for promotion. (To be perceived as a great listener, read the segment titled "Zip your Lips and Listen." Page 128)

Elevator speeches

If you were to attend a PERCEPTIONOLOGY® session, you would be encouraged to give your 30-second elevator speech. For this exercise, you have 30 seconds to introduce yourself, tell us what you do, and tell how we can reach you for business opportunities. The purpose is for you to practice presenting in front of a crowd. The twist to this exercise is that after you are done presenting, you are then given honest feedback from those in attendance as to how we perceived you.

For many of you it might be the first time you hear how you are actually being perceived. I ask the audience if they can remember your name, profession or contact information. I then ask if you made a connection with the group, if you were energetic and sincere. You would also discover the quality of your opening and closing statements. Remember it is not how you perceive yourself but rather how your *audience* perceives you that becomes your reality. Wouldn't it be helpful to hear some honest feedback that could help you improve your skills and be more successful?

The great irony is that most people are willing to share their honest opinion of us with everyone *but* us, especially if it's negative. Yet we are the ones who would benefit the most from that information. The fact is, being denied the truth of how others truly perceive us condemns us to remain unchanged, forever repeating the same critical mistakes that cost us relationships, opportunities, and the ability to make positive changes.

One of the main reasons I started my business was the frustration I felt watching people make interactional mistakes that were negatively affecting how they were perceived. I began challenging people in the course of my daily interactions, asking them why they didn't remember my name when I had just given it to them while stressing the importance of such a skill, and gently reminding them to look me in they eye as I shook their hands.

What pleasantly surprised me was the response I received from most people. They "loved it" and began responding to my constructive criticism. They were actually glad that I told them how I perceived them because no one else was willing to do so. They understood that I was bringing this to their attention because I cared about them as individuals. They would also ask, "What else can you teach me?"

We all like to think of ourselves as sincere, friendly, energetic and professional. If we aren't perceived as such by the people we interact with, then we are none of the above. We all have the ability to change. What most of us are lacking is the awareness that there needs to be a change. You ned to hear the truth as to how your actions are being perceived. Scary… yes. Brutal… possibly. Beneficial… unquestionably!

APPLY THIS IN YOUR LIFE:
Choose someone you know who has the ability to be brutally honest and whose opinion you trust. Make a list of the qualities and skills you feel that you have as a person. Then ask your "evaluator" to critique you based on this list and tell you which areas you need to improve on. You may be surprised about how you are truly perceived.

Track when you practiced these techniques and how it benefitted you.

_____

_____

_____

_____

_____

_____

_____

_____

_____

_____

"Rome wasn't built in a day."

~ *Medieval French proverb*

Quick Fix... There Is None

A lot of people starting their careers, or in professional transition, find out quickly that their circle of influence is not as big as they thought it was. For the first time, they may realize the importance of networking. They may also discover that they are ill-equipped to succeed at it. Networking is a valuable skill that is worth learning to do well.

Successful networking takes time. It involves more than passing out your business card and attending networking functions. There is no networking 'quick fix' because it requires building personal relationships with individuals over time. Furthermore, there are a lot of people who think they're networking when they're actually *not-working*.

Not-working is interacting as if it is all about *you*. It focuses on telling your story and getting others to help you, and it typically offers little to the other person in return. High quality networking isn't about *getting* others to help you; rather, it's about *inspiring* them to help you.

I can't tell you how many times I've gone to a networking function and watched people crash and burn. For example, a person walks up to someone with a business card in hand. This shows a total lack of sincerity. Ideally, your business card should be in someone's hand during the *last* two minutes of your conversation, not the first two minutes. If you instead begin an interaction by asking questions and showing interest in the person you're meeting, you'll be surprised how often the person will in turn ask what you do. That is the moment at which you should hand over your business card. You see, even the simple act of handing out your business card takes a little extra time if you want it to be effective.

The problem is that professionals seeking work often don't feel they have a lot of time to get things going, so they go through the motions of meeting people and collecting business cards. They may not realize that the people they are meeting are sizing them up immediately and perceiving them as insincere. To be successful, all professionals need to realize that they are actually networking during every public moment of their lives.

You have no idea who you will meet today, and who has the power to change your life forever. People will be talking about you, one way or the other. The question is: are they *passing on your name* or merely *passing* on your name? Your networking effectiveness will determine the answer. Furthermore, what you say and do today will in some way impact you tomorrow, for the better or for the worse.

All good things take time
It takes years to build an effective network. Even the phrase *building your network* implies a commitment of effort and time. Although it may be a gradual process, it will pay huge dividends for you if done correctly. A lot of the opportunities that are presenting themselves to me at this time are due to relationships I formed years ago.

I like to try to figure out how some of my opportunities came to be. It's amazing how complicated it gets as I trace back, step by step, the circumstances that led to the final outcome.

Because I want to give my session participants a daily reminder of the importance of presenting themselves to the best of their ability every day, I pass out wristbands after my lectures. The wristbands read "PERCEPTIONOLOGY® HOW YOU ARE PERCEIVED IS YOUR REALITY." They act as a reminder of the learning that has taken place, and help participants stay consciously aware that everyone around them is continuously assessing them. The bands reinforce lessons such as remembering people's names, bringing energy into personal interactions, and offering people their 'best hello.'

The wristbands are white with orange debossed lettering, and over time, they change color. They turn totally orange. It takes several months for this color change to take place. I tell the recipients to observe how the wristbands gradually change color, and I encourage them to give themselves credit for the gradual positive changes in themselves over time.

APPLY THIS IN YOUR LIFE:

Remember that building your network takes time, so be patient and make every personal interaction count. It is better to effectively meet with one or two individuals at a networking event than to try to build relationships with everybody. Take the time to ask questions and learn how you can help others. Review the current contacts in your network and choose someone to call. Ask questions about current status and needs, and find out if there's a person/service/solution you can refer him/her to, or if there is some other way you can help. Practice building your reputation one day at a time and one person at a time.

Track when you practiced these techniques and how it benefitted you.

_____

_____

_____

_____

_____

_____

_____

_____

_____

_____

_____

_____

_____

_____

_____

_____

"Spectacular achievement is always preceded by
unspectacular preparation."

~ *Robert H. Schuller*

"Manners are a sensitive awareness of the feelings of others.
If you have that awareness, you have good manners,
No matter what fork you use."

~ *Emily Postt*

Remember... Lunch Matters

Tips for hosting a business lunch or dinner

Personal and professional relationships are often built or reinforced over lunch. Because you serve as impactful representatives of your company during these face-to-face interactions, you and your employees need to understand the importance of lunch meetings and the value of making a great first impression. I watch people crash and burn on a daily basis when they are interacting with others. Sadly, many never even realize the opportunity they have lost. *You* do not need to crash and burn. Let me help you.

Presentation is everything
While hosting a business lunch/dinner, you are not only showing your guests how professional you are but also how you will treat anyone they refer to you. How you present yourself, what you say and how you say it speaks volumes about you and your company. Every time you open your mouth you are giving a speech, so prepare to be professional and enthusiastic!

How you present yourself visually is also important. For business events, it is always better to over-dress than under-dress. Proper business dress indicates a respect for the guest. Men, you can always remove a tie or sports coat if others are more casually dressed. Ladies, your goal should be to dress in a modest professional style that assures your guest's focus on the business discussion rather than on your attributes.

Your conduct during the meal will also determine your professional success. If you handle the small details correctly and make every effort to see that your clients have a pleasant time, they will assume that you will handle their business affairs the same way.

Be aware that you are constantly being perceived. The good news is; you can positively influence people's perceptions. By incorporating the following simple techniques when hosting a meal, you will set yourself and your company apart from the crowd.

Preparation pays
Know your audience. Think about what you already know, and then learn as many additional facts as you can before you meet with them. Showing a thorough understanding and knowledge of their interests will enhance your credibility during the conversation.

Restaurant prep
Do not make the mistake of meeting at a restaurant that you have not personally tried before. In fact, the best strategy is to go to a restaurant where you already have personal relationships with the staff. Your goal is to stack the deck in your favor, and you do not need any unpleasant surprises. You need to be certain that the food, service and setting will all be conducive to your meeting. Whether the experience is good or bad, it will reflect on you, so make sure it is good.

You are in charge
From the moment you invite your guest, be the one in control. When inviting your guest, rather than saying, "Would you like to join me for lunch?" or "Let's do lunch," you should say, *"I would like to invite you to be my guest for lunch/dinner to discuss [specific business topic]."* This clearly defines who will be in

charge and who is paying the tab. It also allows your guest to prepare for the meeting because he/she clearly understands the topic that will be discussed.

Remember to confirm your appointment with your guest the day before. Everyone is busy and multitasking these days, so don't assume your guest will remember. All the preparation in the world is meaningless if your guest fails to show up. While confirming your meeting, reiterate that you are looking forward to seeing them.

Arrive at least 20 minutes early (more on this below), and please arrive in a car that is clean inside and out. Why: to avoid potential embarrassment. What if you find yourself parked next to your guest, or for some reason need to offer him/her an unplanned ride? Would you have to move a pile of stuff so they can sit in your car? Your car is a direct reflection of you. If your car is filthy, full of trash or in disarray, what does that say about you?

Turn your server into your advocate
You have arrived early, in part so that you can ask the hostess to assign you the best server. Ask for, memorize and use your server's name often. Also make sure your server knows your name, by telling her/him several times. Let your server know this is an important meeting for you and that you picked this restaurant because of the wonderful service the restaurant is known for. Tell your server you understand how essential a great server is for a successful meeting then thank him/her in advance for his/her help.

Because of this advance communication, your server is highly likely to take ownership of your meeting and facilitate it anyway he/she can. A positive relationship with your server will pay big dividends throughout the meal, and can also help assure that your guest doesn't drink more than is safe for them and appropriate for a business meeting.

To alleviate any awkward presentation of the bill, you can arrange ahead of time with your server to not bring the bill to the table. If you trust the restaurant, you can give him/her your charge card to hold, and tell him/her that after the meal you will walk your guest out to his/her car and then will return to settle the bill. It's also wise to remind your server to serve you last; although most servers know this rule, you should not leave it to chance.

Your server can be a tremendous ally at a business luncheon or dinner. Your guest will be noticing how well (or poorly) you communicate with the server, so by being strategic and planning ahead, you are helping to assure a positive perception. And don't underestimate the importance of exceptional service; it can significantly impact the outcome of your meeting.

Any time you are speaking to or thanking your server during the meal, be sure to make eye contact. Even though most people will say they look their server in the eye when addressing them, most servers say that less than 15% of people they are serving ever look them in the eye. Remember, a thank you without eye contact shows no respect and has no value. If you treat your servers with respect they will be encouraged to do their best for you.

There is one exception, however: if your server comes up while your guest is speaking to you, do not take your eyes off your guest until he/she is finished speaking. Remember *while your guest is speaking, he/she is the most important person in the world.* Nothing should distract you from listening to your guest. If you do take your eyes off your guest while he/she is talking, it may feel like a mental face slap to them. In any event, people who walk up to the table will typically wait until you acknowledge them with eye contact before they start talking. If you are the one who is speaking when your server walks up to you, you can feel free to excuse yourself and address the server.

Seating strategy
Another reason for arriving early is to work out the seating arrangements before your guest(s) arrive. Make sure the guests have the best seats… those with a view of the water or skyline, for example. You don't want your guests facing the wall, kitchen or restrooms. Make a mental note of where you will seat each guest. If the table isn't suitable, don't be bashful about asking for a better

one. You have arrived early to control the things you can. Also, round tables work best for parties of five or more. This arrangement allows everyone to see everyone else at all times.

Cell phone etiquette
You should leave your cell phone on in case your guest(s) need to contact you for any reason. Once they arrive, however, remember to turn your cell phone off and consciously raise your energy level. It's show time!

Once your guests arrive, remember you are in charge. You have roughly ten seconds to make an impression, so make it a great one. Stand, walk toward your guests, and greet them with a firm handshake and plenty of eye contact. The simple act of moving toward them will ensure you are perceived as being welcoming.

Names matter
Ask for, memorize and use your guests' names immediately. Most importantly, get the exact pronunciations. Nothing will kill a relationship faster than mispronouncing someone's name over and over again. Do not be afraid to ask them to repeat it if you need to, and make sure you get it right the first time you use it. Immediately use their first name in your initial comments. For example, "Thank you for taking the time to get together today, Robert."

If you need to conduct introductions, rank (title) rules over gender. Use people's proper titles when introducing them. Thank them for coming and let them know you have been looking forward to spending time with them. Address them by name as you direct them to the seats you have already envisioned for them. Also, if your spouse or business partner is with you, use his/her name often so your guests will have an easier time remembering.

Do not sit down until all your guests have been seated. Immediately after sitting down, remove your napkin from the table, open it under the table and place it on your lap. This signals the beginning of the meeting. The only time your napkin should be placed on top of the table again is to signal the end of the meeting, at which time you place it loosely to the left of your plate.

If you must leave the table for any reason, loosely leave your napkin on your chair to signal the server that you will be returning shortly. If you drop your napkin on the floor, do not pick it up; ask your server for a new napkin instead.

First things first: prepare to order

Before starting the conversation, encourage your guest to peruse the menu and decide what they would like to order. Get your orders in and out of the way. This will set the wheels in motion, facilitate the process for your server, and prevent ordering interruptions once a good conversation is going. Good form dictates that you not bring up business until the entrée is finished and the plates removed, so the sooner the meal is served, the sooner you will be able to get down to business. While perusing the menu, make a few suggestions. This suggests the price range and opens the evening to appetizers and a complementary wine (if appropriate). The recommendation can be as simple as, "I've always enjoyed the veal" or "They really are famous for their prime rib."

There are two schools of thought about ordering alcohol. One is proactive: if you order alcohol, other guests will feel free to do so as well. The second is more reactive: you can ask them if they would like a glass of wine or a cocktail before the meal? If your guest declines, then you should also decline, since your goal is to make the guest feel comfortable. If you do order alcohol, you may want to limit the amount that you and your guest consume. Your server can help you do this if you have notified him/her in advance to limit offering more than a certain amount.

Set the tone for the meal

If you intend for guests to order appetizers, then order one yourself. An appetizer gives you the opportunity to 'break bread' together, so order an appetizer that can be shared. Then, remember to let your guests order their entrees first. When it's your turn, avoid ordering messy entrees like finger foods, ribs or spaghetti. You do not want to be worried about food on your face and hands, or drips on your clothing; you have enough to be thinking about as it is. Also, you should order the same number of courses as your guests, since you will not want them to feel uncomfortable because they are eating when you are not.

When your drinks arrive and you feel you want to toast your guest, go right ahead. However, you can also raise a toast to others. For example, I will always remember one gentleman who toasted all those who gave their lives so we at the table could enjoy this fine meal together. This is the beginning of what you hope will be a successful relationship, and it is not about you. By the end of the meal, you want them to know you care about them and you have depth. One more note: if someone toasts you, do not raise your glass or take a drink. If you do, you will be toasting yourself.

Casual conversation do's and don'ts
When you speak, be sure to look at and include everyone who is listening to you at the table. Conversely, when your guest(s) are speaking, *do not take your eyes off the speaker until he/she is finished talking.*

Don't be interesting; be interested
Listening is the nicest thing you can do for someone. Your guests will notice whether or not you are a good listener. If you use your listening skills, by the end of the evening your guests will think they had a wonderful conversation (because it was all about them).

Do not start by talking about yourself. Get the client to start talking about him or herself. For example, you can look for something to comment on. Perhaps a guest is wearing a college ring, special pin or a tie that you can compliment or ask about.

As a guide: you should listen about four times longer than you speak. While listening, look them in the eyes. Lean toward them and ask questions about what they just said. If your guest even looks like they have something to say, stop talking. If you are speaking and your guest starts to talk, be quiet and listen. When someone else is speaking, lean toward them and establish eye contact.

Please note: *If a person stops talking, it doesn't mean you should start talking.* By sitting still and not filling the dead air, you prove to them you are listening. What typically happens next is the person starts talking again, but this time it is on a much deeper level. This listening skill is well worth the effort to learn. Practice this in your everyday life and watch how people respond.

Engage your guest's companion(s)
Do not overlook your client's guest. For example, if your guest brought his/her spouse, call him/her by name and find out some personal details about them. If they are married you can ask the spouse how they first met, or when he/she knew they would marry. Even the spouse will be interested in that answer! When they discuss the evening later, the spouse or guest's opinion will impact the overall perception of the meeting, so make sure you interact meaningfully with him/her.

Avoid one-upmanship
Why is it when we hear a story, we want to tell one that is bigger and better? One of the biggest mistakes you can make, especially in a business interaction, is "outdoing" someone else's story. This is simply the 'kiss of death.' Please don't! You aren't going to win a popularity contest by outdoing your guest. It is not about you. Listen to and ask questions about *their* story instead.

Three great starter questions
1) What are you looking forward to?
Be prepared to hear this question repeated back to you, because people are usually amazed that someone is actually interested in them. It also gives them time to think about their answer. The purpose of this question is to give you a timely and accurate snapshot of a person's present mindset. If someone tells you he/she is not looking forward to anything, then it might not be the best time to try to sell something. Instead, try to simply leave him/her smiling.

If he/she does have something he/she is looking forward to, ask follow-up questions about it. You want to build a relationship, so listen well, ask relevant questions, and Be Truly Interested.™ Your client just handed you the keys to the kingdom; use them. Perhaps it's a vacation, new car, house, child or job. Whatever he/she tells you, take mental notes so you can address it again when saying goodbye.

2) Do you remember your first bike [or other similar question]?
Engage everyone by looking around the table, and start a topic you can all discuss. It should be an ageless question, meaning that people of all ages will be able to respond. You will hear 90 year olds talking as fondly about their first bikes as any teenager. You will be amazed that people want to tell you about their bike. Remember to ask questions along the way, such as: what color was it? Why did you get it? Did it have gears? Did you ever get hurt on it? Where did you like to ride it? For any of us, our bikes represented our first freedom and responsibility, so this simple question can evoke many positive memories.

As people reminisce, they go back in time to when they rode that bike. For a moment they can *become* that child again, without their adult defenses. This can make guests more open to sharing more about themselves. If you notice that faraway look, ask them if they were just riding their bike. Chances are they will say yes. If you listen and ask questions about their first bikes, cars, houses or apartments, for example, by the end of the meal they will feel that you have known them their entire lives.

3) When did you last experience exceptional customer service?
This is a very valuable question. You will be hearing firsthand what your guest(s) feel are important aspects of customer service. In a way, they are telling you what they are expecting from you. By learning what made their service experiences exceptional, you can emulate them to improve your own odds of success.

A little bet
In order to learn more about your guest, ask about his/her interests. Find out what he/she is passionate about and why. If the person has a loyalty to a sports team, you can ask if he/she would like to place a friendly wager on a game (during the Super Bowl almost everyone is willing to place a small wager on the game, for

example). I suggest that you bet two dollars, and hope you lose, for three reasons: first, it keeps the wager friendly; second, if you pay them as soon as the bet ends with a two-dollar bill (available at banks), you are showing you have integrity; third, if and when they spend the two-dollar bill, who do you think will come to mind? Can you see how you just created another potential contact opportunity that can help you build your relationships?

Agree to disagree
In business meetings especially, it is important to respect and *appreciate* other people's opinions. Differences of opinion are what make conversations interesting and enjoyable. How boring would it be if everyone agreed on everything? However, be careful to avoid getting into an argument. It could cost you every ounce of goodwill you have achieved to this point.

Time to eat, Emily Post style
First, a disclaimer: this table manners guidance may seem unnecessary to some of you. However, it has been my experience that we can all benefit from a refresher now and then. These courtesies make the entire eating experience more pleasant in subtle ways.

When the meals arrive, you should be served last. Polite guests will typically wait for the host to begin before starting their own meals. Don't keep them waiting. If it's a small gathering, wait until everyone has been served, then immediately begin eating.

Food should be passed to the right, and you should serve yourself only after everyone else has been served. Items such as salt and pepper holders or cream and sugar bowls should be passed together as a set, and placed by the plate of the person to your right. Remember, when passing teapots, syrup pitchers or gravy boats, to face the handles toward the recipient.

Hold your utensils properly, and use the appropriate utensils for the course being served. In upscale restaurants, the salad forks and soupspoons will be set at the outermost position of the utensil settings. When cutting meat, cut only one piece at a time; do not cut the entire item into pieces at once. When you lay down your knife, it should be placed across the far top of your plate with the blade facing inward. Then, transfer the fork to your other hand before using it to eat. You may also use the European style of cutting, with the fork in your left hand and the tines facing downward. Cut the meat with the knife in your right hand, and then simply raise your fork to your mouth.

Remember that body language is important. Don't slouch towards your plate; bring the food to you instead. To eat bread or rolls, tear one bite size piece off at a time, butter it, and then eat it. It is considered inappropriate to take a bite out of a whole dinner roll, but toast or garlic bread may be eaten as a whole piece.

Avoid eating too fast or too slowly; instead, try to stay in step with your guests so that they won't be eating alone. If you don't like something, just leave it on your plate. If you need to remove an inedible item from your mouth, shield your fork with your free hand as you place the item from your mouth to the fork, and then onto the plate. It is important to be polite and respectful at all times, even if the food or service you are receiving is substandard. Allow time for your guest to eat. When you are finished with your meal, set your knife and fork together on the plate so that both handles are resting at the four o'clock position, and leave your plate exactly where it is. This will signify to your wait staff that you are finished and that your plate can be removed.

Getting down to business
Do not bring up business until the entrée is finished and the plates are removed. If you intend for your guests to order a dessert, you should order one for yourself. Encourage them to order coffee, and then get ready for your business discussion. When drinking coffee, don't bend down to the cup. Rather, be aware of your body language. Sit up straight and bring the cup to your lips, which will give you an air of strength.

As the host, you should be the one to bring up the business to be discussed. Sit up straight and keep your elbows off the table. Since people tend to have short attention spans during these types of meetings and may only retain 20% of what you say, get and keep their attention by keeping your message interesting. Speak well and clearly, gain eye contact around the table, and represent your company well.

Bring energy

Be enthusiastic and look at everyone as you speak. Use hand gestures, modulate your voice, and speak from your heart. Be sincere, and keep it short. Let them know you appreciate what they have done for you so far and look forward to developing your business relationship in the future. Ask them for their thoughts on what you have presented. Appreciate their input even if you have heard it before. The more valued they feel, the more likely it is that they will participate in your plan. Allow time for final questions and thoughts. If they were listening, they will probably have questions for you. You could ask, "What did you hear me say?" The responses might be enlightening, since no two people hear the same thing, even if they are at the same table.

Wrap it up

Please respect your guest's time and conclude the meeting in a timely fashion. When you feel the meeting has come to an end, place your napkin loosely on the table to the left of your plate (not on the plate). This will signal the end of the meeting, so prepare to walk your guest out. As you do, bring up the information you learned at the beginning of the evening, about whatever it is that he/she is looking forward to. Offer good wishes such as "have a great time on that vacation," or "enjoy the new car, house, ..." Remember this personal detail so you can contact them again in the future and ask them about it. It's nice to have a reason other than business to call someone, especially if you intend to strengthen the relationship.

Don't start shaking hands goodbye in the restaurant; you only want to say goodbye once. If they try to shake your hand tell them, "I'm walking you to your car." If they ask about the bill, just tell them matter-of-factly that it's already taken care of, and thank him/her for meeting with you. Walk your guest to his/her car and offer a firm handshake with plenty of eye contact. Say goodbye to each guest individually with a comment. Be the last person to hold eye contact when saying your final goodbye.

Debrief and Critique

Once all of the guests have left, return to the restaurant to pay your bill and thank the wait staff for assisting you. Write down everything and anything you learned about each guest: birthday, anniversary, middle names, kids' names and ages, spouse's name, pets, how they met and what they are looking forward to. Add these to each guest's profile at the next opportunity.

In addition, write down everything you did well and not so well. You are a work in progress. Don't beat yourself up if the meeting didn't go perfectly smoothly. Remember what you did well and improve on your rough spots. If you made your guest(s) feel important, you accomplished the critical goal.

Finally, do not forget to write a thank you card and send it out via 'snail mail' as soon as possible. To make it more personal, place a stamp on the letter rather than using metered postage. When writing your thank you card, remember to use the "YOU" letter format found in the section "You Letters" Will Benefit... YOU! (Page 121)

Track when you practiced these techniques and how it benefitted you.

_____

_____

_____

_____

_____

_____

_____

_____

_____

_____

*Perception*ology®

> *"So let us begin anew... remembering on both sides*
> *that civility is not a sign of weakness*
> *and sincerity is always subject to proof."*
>
> *~ John F. Kennedy*

Sincerity Sets You Apart

If you call me on the phone you will hear me say, "Hello, Donald Wayne McLeod here. How can I help you?" And I mean it. I really want to meet the need of the person on the other end of the line. You are obviously calling me for a reason, and I want to facilitate you as best I can.

We all pride ourselves on our ability to sense if someone is being sincere or not. Being sincerely interested in others is a perceivable way to positively stand out in the crowd. Conversely, trying to form a relationship with someone when you are not being sincere will only set you up for embarrassment and failure. Let me give you an example...

The conversion parable
One of my favorite learning experiences began when two of our neighborhood kids came over to invite my wife and me to their baptism. We try to bond with all of our neighbors and told them we would be happy to attend their special occasion.

When we arrived at their church, we were immediately met by one of six young men being trained for leadership positions. I noticed that he was well dressed and was standing tall. He was employing plenty of eye contact and was smiling as he extended his hand to me and offered me a firm handshake. "Donald Wayne McLeod," I said shaking his firm hand. "Brother Timothy," he replied energetically. "Pleasure to meet you Brother Timothy," I said.

On the surface he seemed to have it all going on. He had energy, used eye contact, had good posture and was well-dressed, and offered a firm handshake and smile. However, sensing something was missing (and while still shaking his hand) I asked, "What's my name?" A huge grin crossed his face as he responded honestly, "I don't have a clue."

I responded, "No, it's not 'I don't have a clue;' my name is Donald Wayne McLeod, and it is a pleasure meeting you Brother Timothy." I didn't do this to embarrass him; I did it because I cared. He was trying to make a great first impression and I wanted him to know that the most important ingredient, being truly interested, was missing. Brother Timothy took it quite well and we did indeed connect in that moment.

Brother Timothy then introduced me to David who was the leader of the church and the person performing the baptisms. I shook David's hand, introduced myself, and told him I was looking forward to the ceremony. My wife and I then entered a room and sat down with the rest of the congregation. It was a moving ceremony and we were genuinely happy to be able to attend.

However, immediately after the ceremony the lights were shut off, the doors were closed and a big screen rolled down out of the ceiling on which a 45-minute video about their religion started playing. Since my wife and I were the only nonmembers of the church, this production was clearly aimed directly at us. Also, there were empty seats deliberately left next to my wife and me. After the video, a woman came over and sat down next to me, looked me in the eye and asked, "What did you think about the video?"

Since I know that the listener controls the conversation (see the segment called "Zip your Lips and Listen"), I turned to her and asked, "Do you have children?" She replied, "Yes, three." "How old are they?" I asked. "Three, five and eight," she responded with a gleam in her eye. "Girls, boys?" I asked, smiling. "The oldest is a boy," she stated proudly. "They must keep you very busy,' I stated. "Absolutely," she nodded. "What is a normal day like for you?" I asked smiling. She smiled back and started telling me about her children.

For the next twenty minutes I listened to her talk about her family. Now remember she was on a mission. I had just watched the baptism and a 45-minute video, and she was supposed to continue softening me up for the kill. But all of that went out the window. Why: because I was sincerely listening to her talk about something that was near and dear to her. She had totally forgotten her purpose for sitting down next to me and was happily telling her personal story to someone who was interested in listening to her.

After twenty minutes my wife and I got up to leave. As we exited the room into the hallway, the six young trainees were now standing like pillars on both sides forming a gauntlet that we were forced to walk through. David was standing at the far end of the hallway and started approaching us so that he would meet us right in the middle of the gauntlet. At this moment the only thing missing was the music you hear preceding a western movie shootout, because we were going to have one, right here and right now.

As David approached me I greeted him with a firm handshake and plenty of eye contact saying, "Great service, David. We are so glad we could be here. What's my name?" David fell silent and shook his head. Brother Timothy spoke up and said, "I remember his name." While still shaking David's hand, I turned to Brother Timothy on my right and said, "Tell David how you remember my name, Brother Timothy." "He made me remember his name," he replied enthusiastically. I turned back to David and sincerely asked him, "How am I supposed to believe you care about my soul when you didn't care enough about me to remember my name?"

Ouch!!! You could have heard the proverbial pin drop, but David proved himself to be a true leader. There was no ego involved. He didn't try to make excuses. He realized that these young men were learning a valuable life lesson and did not want to get in the way of it. David let go of my hand took one step back and asked, "What else can you teach us?"

I told him there were three things they needed to know. First, it is critical to get, remember and use people's names. Secondly, forming a gauntlet to try to force a religious conversion does not work because it made us feel awkward and uncomfortable rather than receptive to their message. Lastly, I told them I was taking my wife to dinner. With that said, they separated like the Red Sea and we walked out of the church. That is the beauty of being the one in control of the conversation!

There are several reasons for telling you this story:
- First, I want you to remember the importance of getting, remembering and using people's names, which is a clear sign of sincere interest.
- Second, as a listener, you have the power to control the conversation and to show your sincere interest in another person. People love to talk about themselves, so take advantage of opportunities to learn about their lives.

- Third, and perhaps most importantly, selling does not happen without sincere caring for others. These people were trying to sell a product: a faith they were so sure of that they were betting their own everlasting lives on it. The product was proven, and the sales pitch was practiced; but they were unable to sell it because they saw me not as a person, but as a nameless conquest.

Each of us is selling a product every day, and that product is *us*. We get to name it, dress it and present it to the best of our ability every day and even if we have imperfect faith in ourselves, if we can authentically connect with others we can sell what we have to offer personally and professionally. However, since people can sense insincerity in others, your efforts must be genuine. Are you a sincere person? If so, it will set you apart and will benefit you personally, financially, and even spiritually.

APPLY THIS IN YOUR LIFE:
The next time you have a conversation with someone, be truly and sincerely interested in what he/she is talking about. See him/her as an individual who wants to be heard, acknowledged and appreciated. Stop thinking about what is in it for you, ask questions about the topic at hand, and focus on whether there is anything you can do for him/her. Observe how your efforts enhance the conversation, and keep track of any short and long-term results from that conversation.

Track when you practiced these techniques and how it benefitted you.

_____

_____

_____

_____

_____

_____

"No one who achieves success does so
without announcing the help of others.
The wise and confident acknowledge this help with gratitude."

~ *Alfred North Whitehead*

"God gave you a gift of 84,600 seconds today.
Have you used one of them to say thank you?"

~ *William Arthur Ward*

Thank You

Throughout this book you'll hear me state that you can accomplish anything if you can inspire others to help you. One of the best ways to inspire others is to express gratitude to those who are helping you already.

My company at one point donated two scholarships for our PERCEPTIONOLOGY® sessions to a local employment agency, to help people who were in transition. The head of the employment agency used one scholarships, and she brought another woman named Kathy, who was client currently in transition, to a session.

One of the first topics we cover is gratitude. So, at this session, I asked all the members of the class to write thank-you letters to someone in their lives. When she heard this, Kathy looked at me, crossed her arms across her chest and matter-of-factly stated that the only person she had to thank was God, and she didn't have his address. I approached Kathy and commented that even though I had only known her for five minutes, I already knew two people she could be thanking. The first person was the woman who told her about this class, and the second person was me, since I provided the scholarship that enabled her to attend. I said that it must be tough getting out of bed every morning believing that no one cares. But the reality was that there were two people within an arm's length of Kathy who were helping her.

It's easy for us to overlook or take for granted the people in our lives who are providing physical, financial, emotional, intellectual, spiritual, or some other kind of support. I want you to be among the people who are paying attention. The purpose of this handbook is to help you stand out from the crowd in a positive way, and that is exactly what will happen when you send a note of appreciation to someone in your life. This is not about thanking people for giving you gifts or for inviting you to a dinner party. I want you to write your thank you letter to sincerely thank someone for helping you through life.

This thank you letter has at least three important benefits. First, it will help you to realize that there are people in your life that you not only *could,* but you *should* be thanking. No man is an island, so this exercise can open your eyes to all those around you who are currently helping you. Secondly, you get the chance to thank these important people, which increases your sense of gratitude and greatly increases the recipients' feelings of goodwill. Thirdly, you may notice that the next time you see that person, the hug is a little tighter, the smile a little brighter, or the handshake a little longer. When you see that what you said meant something special to that person, I hope it will prompt you to send out more letters.

Gratitude is a powerful thing. What happens when someone shows you sincere gratitude for something that you have done for them? Exactly; you want to help them even more. They have *inspired* you to want to help them.

Before you write the thank you letter, read the section on writing 'You Letters.' Remember it should be handwritten and hand-stamped. Do not send thank you letters through your metered mail. You want everything about it to be personal. Open your eyes to those who are helping you personally and professionally, and express your gratitude for the help. It will benefit them – and *you.*

APPLY THIS IN YOUR LIFE:
Create a running list of the people in your personal and professional lives that you could and should thank for their help and support. Write those thank-you letters using the format found in the segment titled "You Letters." Leave space by each name to make notes on the short and long-term results of your notes of gratitude, and how they have benefitted you. Continue to add to the list as more people enter your life and are inspired to help you.

Track when you practiced these techniques and how it benefitted you.

_____

_____

_____

_____

_____

_____

_____

_____

> "I know that you believe you understand
> what you think I said, but I'm not sure you realize
> what you heard is not what I meant."

~ *Robert McCloskey*

Understand This: We Do Not Understand

"I saw a box in the street the other day." You may think you understand this. The fact is, we often are only pretending we understand what someone is telling us, and vice versa. In reality, no one fully understands anyone else.

During a live presentation, I will often say to the audience, "I saw a box in the street the other day. Are there any questions?" No one ever asks me a question about that sentence. So I ask the participants, "What's the box made of?" Sometimes people say the box is made out of cardboard, others say wood or some other material. Now I'm asking you the reader, "What do you think the box is made of?"

My box vs. your box
I then walk around the room, asking the following questions: (please take your time and try answering these questions yourself.) "How big is the box?" "Is there writing on it?" "What does it say?" "What's in the box?" "How did the box get there?" "What kind of street is it?" "Where in the street is the box?" "Is it in danger of being hit?" "What kind of day is it?" "How are you seeing the box? Are you walking or driving?" "If you're driving, what are you driving?"

The amazing thing is that each and every person I ask can give me answers to these questions, as can you. We each take what we hear and place it into our own realm of experience and context, and that's what determines the sentence's meaning for us.

People are able to tell me how the box got there, what's in it, and if it was a sunny, rainy or snowy day. They can describe what they were wearing when they saw the box. If they were driving, they cannot only tell me what kind of vehicle they are driving but how much gas is in the tank. Interestingly, they are not making it up. They are consciously thinking about what that sentence meant to them.

This is exactly what we do with everything we hear every day. My box in the street the other day meant something totally different to me than how you visualized it.

The key to communication is asking questions. If you want to truly understand what someone is saying, you must gather more detail. Ironically, many people believe that asking questions implies that they were not listening, but actually the converse is true. When we ask questions, we are showing a person that we are truly interested in understanding them. When I ask a speaker, "Who was your best listener," he/she almost always says it was the person who asked questions.

Square/circle/triangle
Another example I have used to demonstrate our inability to fully communicate with one another is called the square, circle and triangle exercise. I warn the audience that this is going to be frustrating for them. Then I draw a square that intersects a circle and triangle on a blank piece of paper. I then choose an audience member to come up and explain the drawing to the group so that the others can draw the diagram exactly as the person describing it sees it.

The person describing the drawing can only use verbal communication to describe the diagram. The audience is familiar with the concept of the exercise and knows they can ask questions. How many questions do you think they will need to ask before they're able to draw a square, circle and triangle exactly the way I drew it? Would ten questions be sufficient? Perhaps twenty would do the trick? Would 30 be too many?

What usually happens is, the describer tells the audience to draw a square. I watch as the majority of the participants look at their papers and start to draw squares. No one has asked how big the square should be. In fact, it is often not until the 10th or 11th question that the matter of size even comes into play. I often have to remind the audience that asking questions is not a bad thing. I then tell them to pretend that the person describing this diagram is a client that I've referred to them, and my selling point was that they really pay attention and try to understand what a client is saying.

Once the audience understands the new professional scenario, the questions start to fly. Where on the paper is it? What color ink was used? Is the paper portrait or landscape? Is it a perfect square? How big is the circle compared to the square? I usually have to stop the exercise after 50 questions have been asked. I have yet to see anyone draw the square, circle and triangle exactly as it was originally drawn.

If you believe you would be able to describe this type of diagram accurately, I encourage you to try. Draw a simple square, circle and triangle intersecting on a blank piece of paper and then describe it to a group of friends and/or family members without showing it to any of them. It's a frustrating but excellent demonstration that we don't ever understand one another completely.

The point of the exercise is this: if we can't get people to understand a basic square-circle-triangle image, how are we ever going to help them understand our more complex thoughts, concepts and ideas? When describing something to other people, words alone will not get the job done. We need to be very creative and paint a picture for them, and to encourage questions to provide more details.

Part of the challenge is that people typically listen in 'black and white;" meaning, with limited attention, imagery and energy. When was the last time you told someone something and they followed it up with a question? Do you really think they understood what you were telling them? For that matter, when was the last time you listened actively to someone else and asked insightful follow-up questions?

Set yourself apart from the black-and-white crowd. Start listening in color. Start asking thoughtful questions. Become truly interested in the communication of others. It will benefit you in every area of your life. If you want to improve your communication and have others remember you, make the effort to find out more about their 'boxes.'

APPLY THIS IN YOUR LIFE:
When someone tells you something today, start listening in color. Ask at least three follow-up questions about whatever it is that they tell you. Notice how much more information you receive and how much better you understand the topic. The person you ask will be glad to fill in the details and will be pleased that you care enough to ask. Take notes on how much more you have learned from, and about, this person.

Track when you practiced these techniques and how it benefitted you.

_____

_____

_____

_____

_____

_____

_____

_____

_____

_____

_____

"Opportunity is missed by most people because
it is dressed in overalls and looks like work."

~Thomas Jefferson

Value Your Contact Opportunities

Positive points of contact are a necessary main ingredient for building
interpersonal relationships. A positive point of contact happens when you
connect with others in a meaningful and personal way, with no hidden
agenda, meaning you are not selling anything nor are you asking for
anything in return. In order to develop these all-important positive points
of contact, you need to to reach out and touch people in positive,
personal ways as frequently as possible, without it feeling forced.

Get some details

A great way to create positive points of contact is to learn about the
personal lives of those with whom you want to build better relationships.
Do they have children? What are their names? Are they active in local
sports that you can follow? Are they in the school's marching band or in
the high school plays? Are they in the Girl Scouts? Think they would
like you to purchase tickets to the play or order some cookies? There is
not a lot that people are more interested in than their own children, so by
becoming sincerely interested in them, you will easily develop positive
points of contact. If you know these details, you can also congratulate the
parents when their kids are recognized for an accomplishment such as
making the honor roll, the basketball team or the cheerleading squad.

Use sports to your advantage

Do you know what amateur, college or professional sports teams your
friends/colleagues/clients root for? You could drop someone a
congratulatory email after his/her team wins a World Series, Super Bowl,
or national or high school championship. As I write this book, a Super
Bowl is about to take place. What a perfect time for me to create positive
points of contact as I congratulate all the winning fans in my network
and console all the losing fans as well. What a valuable connection
opportunity!

Do you think anyone else was doing this? Based on the responses I
received from those I contacted, the answer is no. They were all grateful
and willing to talk about their teams. Some wrote long notes back to me

regarding their teams and their chances for next year. This common ground was a great channel through which I could connect.

Bet on positive contacts
A small wager can be another great way to connect with someone. For example, during the Super Bowl a lot of people are willing to wager on the outcome of the game. To create a positive point of contact, keep the wager friendly and small – just a dollar or two. Remember it isn't the amount of the bet that is important; you simply want a reason to contact that person again.

When you make the bets, hope that you lose. This will give you the chance to contact these folks and demonstrate you are a person of integrity. When you see them, enthusiastically congratulate them on their big wins and pay them with crisp new money.

In fact, I purposefully make two-dollar bets for several reasons:
- It keeps the bet friendly.
- It allows me to make the payoff seem special by giving or sending brand new two-dollar bills that I get from my bank.
- People tend to hold on to two-dollar bills, but if and when they spend them; guess whose name will come to mind?
- You have created an opportunity to contact someone in a fun and positive manner. What if you win the bet and the other person doesn't pay you? Since the purpose of this exercise was to create goodwill, do not make a big deal out of it. At worst, you have learned some valuable information about the other person's integrity.

Object lesson
There are opportunities to personally connect with those around you on a daily basis. Recently I was facilitating a dinner event for a local city's chamber of commerce. There was a trade show being held in a few weeks, and the dinner was being used to gather and encourage the participating companies to put their best foot forward during the exhibition. I was going to be speaking to the group for over an hour about how to present themselves and how to get the most out of the trade show.

As always, I arrived early to observe how the participants presented themselves and interacted. Most people came in and quickly sat down at a table. You would have sworn they were glued to their chairs – no one was getting up to mingle or meet new people. Those who did come up to meet me started talking about themselves and their companies immediately, which, if you have been reading this handbook, you know is not the way to succeed at networking.

Meanwhile, I was meeting people at nearby tables by getting, remembering and using their names. As the restaurant started filling up, I purposely walked to the front of the restaurant and started welcoming people individually as they came in (coincidentally, the next five people I greeted were women). I welcomed them with energy and got their names. I asked if they knew where they were going to sit. When they said no, I offered to find each one a seat.

I walked them back to the tables with the people whose names I now knew. I introduced the ladies to everyone sitting at that table. I took their coats and let them know where I would be hanging them. I pulled out their chairs for them. Every one of them was grateful that I had given them my professional attention, remembered their names, and introduced them to the people they would be eating with. They appreciated the special treatment, and it showed in how they interacted with me.

As I returned to the front of the restaurant to welcome arriving people, the executive director of the chamber asked if I was the maître d'. The unkind comment didn't bother me because it meant that she had noticed my extra effort, and so had the rest of the group. I had recognized the opportunity to create positive points of contact with the attendees and had acted on it. I understood how uncomfortable it might be walking into a meeting where the guests might not know anyone else. Believe me, the women I welcomed appreciated my 'hosting,' and that in turn helped me achieve positive points of contact with several new people.

Everyone sitting in the restaurant could have done what I was doing, but none of them recognized or valued that opportunity. They were content to maintain their apathy and stay invisible. If you want to successfully grow your network, your business or your circle of influence, you need to meet new people. Don't just sit in your seat with the people you already know. Step out of your comfort zone and become aware of the available opportunities to create positive points of contact with those around you, in any situation.

Value your social media opportunities
Speaking of growing your network, how many connections do you have in your LinkedIn professional network? When was the last time you connected with any of them? Having 500 people on your list doesn't mean you have 500 people willing to help you. What it does mean, however, is that you have 500 opportunities for positive points of contact. The next time you have some free time, send messages through LinkedIn to some of the people in your network. LinkedIn sends you updates about your contacts, such as their profile updates, promotions, work anniversaries, new connections and new jobs, and these can provide great contact points. A simple message of congratulations or "I've been thinking about you – how is it going?" is all it takes.

You will be surprised at the responses you receive. I have sometimes received full pages back from those I reach out to. You can also recommend the skills of the contacts you know, or write a personal endorsement for someone, which keeps your site, and theirs, active and visible. (One caution – these must be authentic endorsements and recommendations. If you don't know about their skills, don't recommend them, or your activity will be received negatively.) People generally appreciate making a connection and want to feel that someone out there is interested in their abilities and accomplishments. Reach out to your professional network by developing authentic positive points of contact through social media, and watch your sphere of influence and support grow exponentially.

Back at ya, Donald Wayne
While traveling to Columbus to deliver a lecture, I stopped at my usual gas station two hours from home to fill up and get my favorite Starbucks coffee drink. After filling up my truck in the freezing cold I was looking forward to stepping inside the warm building and ordering my usual beverage. As I walked into the building a young lady was looking right at me. "Didn't you see me? I was pounding on the glass," she said. "You're Donald Wayne McLeod. Did you come to get your Venti Mocha Frappuccino with three extra pumps of mocha, extra ice, chocolate whip and drizzle?" I said, "Yes, please." Running through my mental contact file, I said, "I know your name begins with an M." I guessed Melissa or Melanie, and she said, "It's Megan."

I had met Megan briefly three months earlier, and I remembered that it was a great meeting. I had commented on her posture, energy and great hello. I wanted to encourage her, and because of our interaction she remembered the meeting, my favorite drink, and me. Had I been on my game and looked up 'Starbucks' on my phone I would have seen her name, because I put it in there after our last meeting. I wanted to remember her as well. I will never forget it again. She said she wanted to make my drink, and went behind the counter where three other people were preparing beverages. Megan wasn't going to let anyone else make my coffee. I walked out of there feeling like a million bucks. Someone wanted to go out of her way for me because we had had a positive point of contact earlier in time. Thank you, Megan.

Every time you meet someone you have an opportunity to create a positive point of contact. Remember and use the concepts you have read here. Get, remember and use names, bring energy to your interactions, and be excited about meeting others. Use eye contact, smile, encourage, send thank you notes, give kudos, and be willing to step out of your comfort zone to meet new people.

Positive points of contact can also become traditions that maintain relationships over time. For example, my wife and I have enjoyed a twenty-year tradition by establishing a friendly Monday Night Football 'point of contact' with another couple. Each week during the season we take turns calling each other up to set the spread for that week's game. In case of a tie, the person setting the spread wins. We continue to play until one of us wins nine games or more than half of the 17 games played during the season. The bet is a dinner out for the four of us, paid for by the loser of the bet, at whatever restaurant the winners select. The benefits to both couples are that we have a reason to keep in touch over the winter months, and that we have the opportunity to enjoy some amazing restaurants that we might not have experienced otherwise. It also makes Monday Night Football games exciting to watch!

APPLY THIS IN YOUR LIFE:
Take note of personal details you learn about your connections. Look for opportunities to congratulate them or console them, and to be appropriately supportive of their interests. The next time you are in a networking atmosphere, make sure you meet or greet at least one new person. Introduce him/her to someone you know. Log into your LinkedIn account and start sending short messages to your connections, especially those you haven't connected with in a while. As you go through your days, develop a new habit of keeping your eyes open for opportunities to create positive points of contact.

Track when you practiced these techniques and how it benefitted you.

_____

_____

_____

_____

_____

_____

_____

_____

_____

_____

_____

"Every time you open your mouth you are giving a speech. Act like it!"

~ Donald Wayne McLeod

"Whoever guards his mouth and tongue keeps his soul from troubles."

~ Proverbs 21:23

What You Say Says a Great Deal… About You!

I am a Cleveland Cavaliers fan who follows my team in the news media. I remember hearing a rookie named LeBron James on the radio saying, "I just want the fans to come out and see how much better we is." When I heard him say that I cringed. My first thought was, who edited that clip? Surely they knew that was improper English and that it would reflect poorly on LeBron. Fortunately, he has come a long way in his speaking performance.

Although he is tremendously gifted with athletic ability, sponsors would not continue to be associated with LeBron James if he continued to speak poorly. What sponsors are looking for is someone with athleticism and intelligence who can represent them credibly. LeBron understood that. I believe he has been working with a speech coach, because more recently I heard an improved LeBron speaking to reporters after co-hosting the ESPN ESPY Awards with Jimmy Kimmel.

A speech coach might tell you to avoid using the word 'good.' You don't play *good*, you don't feel *good*… you play *well*, you feel *well*. It seemed as if LeBron was listening to that coach when he was asked how he felt about co-hosting the event with Jimmy Kimmel. His comment was, "Jimmy could have hosted the event all by himself because he is just that well." A little slip-up, but you can tell he is seriously working on his verbal game.

Kudos to LeBron for taking his own words seriously. He has become a high profile spokesperson and has elevated every part of his game, including how he speaks, to a higher level. LeBron understands that he is a product and a marketing machine, and that what he says speaks volumes about him as a person and an athlete. He also understands that to secure endorsement deals he needs to present himself as a professional.

The same is true about you. Although you may not be negotiating million-dollar endorsement deals, you are still being observed and evaluated by everyone around you. Every time you open your mouth you are giving a speech, so it's important to act like it. One of the primary factors that determine how people perceive you is your use of language.

How you speak is just as important as what you say. Your energy, conviction, modulation, word choices and diction matter a great deal. Do you invest energy into your conversations and presentations? Do you speak with confidence? Do you engage your audience with appropriate volume and interactive questions? Do you use negative terms, or speak in a monotone? Do you slur your words or keep inserting phrases such as 'uh, 'like,' 'you know,' and 'man'?

Behavior determines reception and perception

It is important to mention that your actions and behaviors as you speak matter as well. For example, do you stand when you are meeting someone? If you don't, you're telling the person that he/she isn't important enough to stand for. This does not go unnoticed.

When people are talking to you, do you look in their eyes or do you look around the room? If someone is talking to you and you don't give him/her eye contact, you can be perceived as a person who is not trustworthy.

When you thank someone, do you look him/her directly in the eyes? Remember that a thank you without eye contact means absolutely nothing. Ironically, we do it to family members and service providers on a daily basis. Keep that in mind the next time a waitress pours you a cup of coffee.

Are you a gossip? The fact is, if you are talking about someone else to me, I know you're also talking about me to someone else. What does that say about your trustworthiness?

Your mother was right – appearances matter. If you are in a networking or business environment, are you dressed like a professional or do you look like someone getting ready to change the oil in your car? Remember, if you want to be perceived as a professional, you must look the part.

Your posture is also an important nonverbal communication channel. Are you walking tall with a sense of energy and confidence, or do you walk with your shoulders hunched over and your eyes down, showing doubt and insecurity? Self-defense and martial arts courses teach men and women to stand tall and walk with a sense of power and confidence, so that they're not seen as easy prey in public places. These habits would also serve communicators well.

Attitudes attract or repel

People know about us only what we tell them. Unfortunately, we 'tell' people more about who we are by our attitudes than we do verbally. What are your attitudes telling others about you? Are you someone who:

- Is always running late?
- Always has to be right?
- Criticizes others?
- Respects other people's opinions?
- Admits when you're wrong?
- Forgives others?
- Is a good sport?
- Is a good listener?
- Is a know-it-all or can learn something new?
- Is honest, friendly, passionate, trustworthy, compassionate or charismatic?
- Is arrogant, needy, negative, insincere, boring, unfriendly or selfish?

All the above perceptions of us are based on our attitudes and the behaviors that result from them. We typically don't perceive ourselves as others perceive us. Do people who never shut up realize that they never shut up? If they did, do you think they would continue to behave in this counterproductive way? They don't see this negative trait in themselves. Unfortunately, others are rarely willing to share what they perceive, especially if the perception is negative. Instead, they will just try to avoid those people.

If I asked you to give me the name of the most energetic person you know, would you be able to do it? If I asked you to identify the friendliest or most athletic person you know? You could fill in the blank. But you could also identify the most negative person, or the biggest bore, or the least sincere person you know. My point here is that everyone we know can fill in those blanks. Into which categories are your friends, family, colleagues or clients putting your name?

The good news is that you can turn this around. You can actively influence how people perceive you. If you want to be perceived as a great conversationalist, then learn to ask questions that will engage the person you're conversing with. If you want to be perceived as a positive, energetic and friendly individual, then consciously act positive, energetic and friendly. If you want to be perceived as a confident and sincere business professional then start acting like one.

APPLY THIS IN YOUR LIFE:
What you say and how you say it has a huge impact on how others perceive you. Select a characteristic you would like to work on improving (friendliness, graciousness, promptness, trustworthiness) and practice the behaviors that will allow others to perceive this characteristic in you. For example, decide that every time you see a new face in a group, you will be the first to introduce yourself and show your friendliness by asking a question of them. Or, that you will start watching the clock more closely and be early or on time for every date and appointment from here on. Make a note of any positive change in the reactions of others.

Track when you practiced these techniques and how it benefitted you.

---

*"The more often we do something wrong,
the less wrong it becomes."*

~ The Diminishing Law of Transgression

X Marks The Do's And Don'ts

This entire segment is actually a tool you can apply to reinforce the key lessons in this handbook. It's a way to help keep you on track to becoming your best personal and professional self. Review the focus areas in the tables below, and then make a special effort to focus on one area in your personal and/or professional life until you have incorporated (do's) or eliminated it (don'ts). Once you feel you have mastered a philosophy or skill, check it off. Add notes to remind you about how you achieved it, or how you can maintain it.

Once you have mastered everything on these do and don't lists, use them as reminders and references as you need them. We all need knowledge refreshment every now and then!

Track when you practiced these techniques and how it benefitted you.

_____

_____

_____

_____

_____

_____

_____

_____

_____

_____

PERCEPTIONOLOGY® Do's		
Item	Notes	Done?
DO prepare mentally Remember: 1. You are not alone – we are all in the same boat 2. You are being perceived every waking moment 3. You have a lot of control over how others perceive you 4. You are continually branding yourself through your presentation 5. You are the product. Before you can sell your ideas, products, or services, you must first sell yourself 6. *Two seconds* is all it takes to endear yourself 7. Your goal is to *inspire* others to want to help you 8. Others only know what you 'tell' them with words and actions 9. FEAR stands for Fantastic Energy Always Ready 10. Continue to seek your life's passions 11. When you meet one person, you are also meeting everyone they know 12. Everyone likes to tell their story 13. Someone you meet today could change your life 14. Believe in yourself and your abilities		

PERCEPTIONOLOGY® Do's		
Item	Notes	Done?
DO assure that you are memorable 1. Introduce yourself effectively 2. Always offer your best "Hello" 3. Be interest*ing* and interest*ed* 4. Ask questions and gather personal details 5. Use someone's middle name when appropriate 6. Be entertaining 7. Offer a great goodbye		
DO make sure you're effective 1. Get, remember and use people's names 2. Get the proper pronunciation and spelling of people's names 3. Look at everyone you are speaking to 4. Stand to introduce yourself 5. Present your business card during the last two minutes of the conversation, preferably after it's requested		

PERCEPTIONOLOGY® Do's		
Item	Notes	Done?
DO act graciously		
1. Acknowledge others and make them feel important		
2. Offer kudos and compliments whenever appropriate, to people of all ages and stations		
3. Say "please" and "thank you" often, and say "thank you" rather than "thanks"		
4. Look at the person when you thank them		
5. Remember to include others in conversation		
6. Respect and appreciate others' opinions		
7. Say, "I appreciate *you*," not "I appreciate it"		
8. Build relationships by joining in on activities others are interested in		

PERCEPTIONOLOGY® Do's		
Item	Notes	Done?
DO be a powerful communicator		
1. Nurture your contacts and build your network every day		
2. Set up an automated email signature block with all your contact information and a 'thumbnail' head shot		
3. Send personally written thank you notes		
4. Remember that every time you open your mouth you are giving a speech		
5. Remember that the listener controls the conversation, so direct the conversation with your questions		
DO be consistent and in control		
1. Bring energy to your interactions		
2. Employ good eye contact		
3. Keep your eyes on their eyes when shaking someone's hand		
4. Wear your name badge to make it easy for people to remember your name		
5. Be the last person holding eye contact when saying goodbye		
6. Always be a professional		

PERCEPTIONOLOGY® Don'ts		
Item	Notes	Done?
DON'T turn people off **Do not:** 1. Criticize 2. Pre-judge others 3. Be a know-it-all 4. Expect payback for anything you do for others		
DON'T be a poor conversationalist **Do not:** 1. Talk more than you listen 2. Monopolize the conversation 3. Gossip about others 4. Outdo someone else's story		
DON'T be rude **Do not:** 1. Look around when shaking hands 2. Look around, or at your watch/phone, when listening to others 3. Interrupt others 4. Talk over others		

PERCEPTIONOLOGY® Don'ts		
Item	Notes	Done?
DON'T perform poorly **Do not:** 1. Fake sincerity 2. Shake or squeeze someone's hand too hard when meeting them 3. Use filler words or sounds in your speech 4. Say, "I am really nervous" when addressing an audience (translation: " I am not responsible for anything coming out of my mouth." 5. Forget you are influencing others positively or negatively all the time		
DON'T let others hold you back **Do not:** 1. Underestimate your incredible ability to encourage others 2. Allow others to discourage you 3. Be afraid to be different 4. Be afraid to grab the spotlight when appropriate 5. Stop learning 6. Forget that *you matter*		

"I believe that as much as you take, you have to give back. It's important not to focus on yourself so much."

~ Nicole Kidman

'You Letters' Will Benefit... You!

In our written communications we have a tendency to apply the first person (I, me, my) quite often. We tend to be writing from our own perspective, so it feels natural and seems to read correctly to us. However, we are not the end-user of the message. We need to focus on the readers of these communications, and on writing the letter so that it engages them.

I challenge you to take a look at one of your recently written communications, and count how many times you employ the first person in it. If the number is high, don't beat yourself up about it – many of us do the same thing when we're not being purposeful in our writing. Fortunately, by learning the skills in this section, you can become a more effective writer and change the way you communicate with others for the better.

Here is a sample of a typical thank you card. Read it as if you are the recipient.

Dear Sarah,

I wanted to say thanks for inviting me to the dinner party. I truly appreciated the opportunity to meet some new and interesting people.

By the way, I loved the Death by Chocolate dessert. Thanks again, I enjoyed myself thoroughly and hope we can get together again soon.

Sincerely,

Joan

This seems like a nice enough thank you note, and the mere fact that Joan sent it will separate her from the crowd. However, in this example, there are six references to *me*, *myself* and *I* with no references to Sarah by using *you* or your. A 'thank you' card really should keep the 'you' in mind.

Whether you are writing a thank you note or a business letter, remember to make it a "You Letter." Avoid referring to yourself (*I*, *me*, *my*, *myself*) unless it's necessary. Instead, find ways to keep the focus on the recipient/reader by using *you*, *your* and *yours* wherever appropriate.

Here's another note for your consideration:

> *Dear Sarah,*
>
> *Thank you for the invitation to your dinner party. You truly are a wonderful hostess. Thank you also for the opportunity to meet your diverse and interesting friends.*
>
> *By the way, Sarah, your Death by Chocolate dessert was just that – "to die for." Thank you again, my friend, for a wonderful evening.*
>
> *Sincerely,*
>
> *Joan*

Notice how the whole dynamic of the letter changed? In this example there are 11 references to the reader as a wonderful hostess (even the term 'my friend' refers to Sarah). This style of writing allows you to place the focus on the reader, in this case, the person you want to thank.

This you-focused style of writing should be used for every written communication. However, a cover letter for a job application may be one of the most important communications to craft in this way. Most people read a three-line advertisement in the paper or a few sentences on the Internet, and believe they know what a job entails. They want to tell the company all about their skills and capabilities, and why they are the right person for the job, so they tend to use first person a lot in these letters.

The fact is, keeping the communication focused on the job and the company, instead of on you, shows a true interest in the position.

The following is part of an actual letter sent to me by a woman interested in the executive director position at a company we will refer to as "Acme, Inc." Because she knew this was my area of expertise, she asked if I would look it over and make changes as needed. Notice the focus of this original letter.

Dear Mr. Brown:

*I read **your** job posting for the executive director of Acme, Inc. on May 24th with utmost interest and **I** believe that **my** experience and education will make **me** a competitive candidate for this position.*

*You will find **me** to be personable, detail-oriented and confident in **my** ability to work with numbers and standard operating procedures. **I** am also willing to learn additional abilities necessary to perform **my** duties through the Non-Profit and Public Service Center with Lakeland Community College.*

*   *I met Jessica Rose during one of our Coalition meetings recently and she informed **me** that they have an excellent program that offers professional development classes for non-profit agencies such as Acme, Inc.*

*I hope that you'll find **my** experience and interests intriguing enough to warrant a face-to-face meeting, as **I** am confident that **I** would be an asset to this wonderful organization that helps so many underprivileged individuals in securing their piece of the American dream of home ownership.*

*I look forward to hearing from you and **I** thank you for your consideration.*

Sincerely,

Jennifer Smith

With the exception of the conclusion, the focus on the writer far outweighs the focus on the reader, job and company, with a three-to-one ratio of 18:6.

After receiving this letter, I spent four hours revising it in the hopes of securing her at least a personal interview. Here is another version:

Dear Mr. Brown:

*If **you** had been watching me read **your** posting for the position of executive director of Acme, Inc., **you** would have seen my excitement. **You** need to know that a candidate with strong administrative and leadership skills has found **you**. Hopefully **you** can feel my sincere interest in the opportunity **you** are presenting.*

*Mr. Brown, I am interested in hearing about the direction **you** have in mind for Acme, Inc. It's important to me, as a professional and a community member, to learn about **your** goals, **your** vision and **your** future plans for the organization. **You** will find me to be a good listener.*

***Your** next executive director will need more than excellent writing skills; she will also need to exhibit exceptional people skills. It is difficult to convey my interpersonal expertise to **you** through this letter, Mr. Brown, but if we have an interview, **you** will discover a candidate with leadership abilities who is capable of molding **your** staff of individuals into a productive team. **You** will be conversing with someone who truly believes that nothing affects our daily lives more than our ability to interact with others effectively.*

*Thank **you**, Mr. Brown, for offering this amazing career opportunity. I look forward to meeting **you** to discuss **your** ideas, **your** strategies, and **your** expectations for the executive director role.*

Sincerely,

Jennifer Smith

In this revision, there is an approximately one-to-three ratio with 8 *me's to 22 you's*. Notice how the emphasis has shifted from the writer to the reader. Stating that Jennifer wants to hear his goals, his vision and his future plans for Acme Inc. shows her true desire to understand the position. It also shows the kind of leadership qualities he would be looking for in an executive director.

I sent the revised letter to Jennifer later the next day. She let me know that she had already sent in her original letter, and then called me two days later proud to tell me that the organization had notified her that they had received her resume. What I wanted to tell her was that she had just received the "don't-call-us-we'll-call-you" phone call, but I kept it to myself. In the end, she was not granted an interview. She now has a far less desirable job and wonders what went wrong.

Ironically, this story relates to one of the concepts that comes up often in this handbook – "it's not about you." Although I spent four hours rewriting Jennifer's cover letter, with the goal of helping only her, the writing lesson I eventually developed from it has become the most requested PERCEPTIONOLOGY PowerPoint presentation to date (and now a chapter in this book). The lessons it offers have helped thousands of individuals and hopefully thousands more. In retrospect, those may have been among the most productive hours of my life!

Getting it done step-by-step
I don't expect you to become an expert at writing the You Letter overnight. It's a skill that requires practice. Here are some guidelines to keep in mind as you write You Letters:

1. Instead of the word 'thanks,' always use 'thank you.' Keep in mind we want to add as many *you's* as we reasonably can, and this rule will help.

2. Try to replace the word 'the' with 'your' wherever it makes sense. You will be surprised how often you can apply this rule.

3. See if you can replace the word 'my' with 'the,' or better yet, 'your.' Remember, we are not only trying to add *you's* but we are trying to remove 'me,' 'my,' and 'mine.'

4. People not only like hearing their names, they like reading them as well. Use the reader's name at least once in the body of every written communication.

Here are examples of rewriting a sentence to improve the 'you' focus. Note how the me-to-you ratio changes with each revision:

1. I have attached my proposal for the project to this email. (2:0)

2. I have attached my proposal for your project to this e-mail. (2:1)

3. I have attached the proposal for your project to this e-mail. (1:1)

4. You will find the proposal for your project attached to this e-mail. (0:2)

5. David, you will find the proposal for your project attached to this e-mail. (0:3).

Writing the You Letter is a step-by-step process. Review your sentences several times to see how if you can improve them to reflect the 'you' focus. This will not only change the way you communicate with others; it will change the way others respond to you.

There is also a place for I and me

Writing the I Letter
There is one time when the attention should be on you... can you guess when that would be in order? The letter below demonstrates a situation in which you should refer to yourself as often as possible:

> *Dear Kathy,*
>
> *I owe you **my** apology. **I** was wrong, and **I've** learned a valuable lesson from this mistake. **I** will be sure to double-check **my** billing in the future. Again, please accept **my** apology. **I** appreciate your understanding.*
>
> *Sincerely,*
>
> *Nathan Alan*

Can you see how the use of "I" and "my" shifts the attention onto the writer? Nathan Alan is accepting responsibility and showing integrity by doing so. In this case, the writer takes the attention; but in most written communication he/she should not.

APPLY THIS IN YOUR LIFE:

Review some of your most recent correspondence. Count how many times you used first-person pronouns, as opposed to referring to the reader(s). Try rewriting these letters by applying the lessons in this segment. Before you send out your next written communication, check the ratio of 'I's' to 'you's' in your draft. Also make sure that you have used the person's name at least once in the body of the letter.

Track when you practiced these techniques and how it benefitted you.

_____

_____

_____

_____

_____

_____

_____

_____

_____

_____

_____

_____

"We have two ears and one mouth,
so that we can listen twice as much as we speak."
~ *Epictetus*

Zip Your Lips And Listen!

How many people do you know? In my lectures, the typical response to this question is, "I know a lot of people and a lot of people know me." Surprisingly, people don't usually ask a follow-up question before answering. A good follow-up question would be "what do you mean by 'know'?" By asking that question, they might have understood my first question more clearly.

Then I ask my next question, "How many people know you?" Now I see people starting to really think about this. The question has now taken on a much deeper meaning. They start to look at it from a different perspective. I tell them I want them to take that question to the nth degree. "How many people really, really know you? When you think you truly understand the question, take it one step further."

I open up my hands and bring them around to the front of my face, palms facing me. I say, "We went from 'I know a lot of people' to 'how many people really know me?'" I look at the group as I start curling my fingers into fists one at a time until I have only one extended. At this point, I tell the group that I believe I can ask them a question about themselves that they cannot answer.

I then ask the participants to take a look around the room and realize that we are all in the same boat. While everyone is nodding their heads in agreement I ask them, "Why is it that no one knows us?"

It is my opinion based on my years of experience with interpersonal relations that people don't know us because they are not willing to listen. Think about this... when was the last time someone listened intently to you? These days, the only time we typically experience this type of listening is when we are paying hundreds of dollars an hour and lying on a couch.

There is a big difference between 'knowing' someone and deeply, personally knowing him/her, and the only way to really get to know a person is by asking relevant and thoughtful questions. The next time you walk into a room full of people, realize that each and every one of them would love to have someone listen to them. Since I understand this fact, I have no problem walking up to anyone, anyplace, anytime, and starting a conversation with him/her.

Listening is such a rare occurrence these days that the mere effort to be a good listener will make you stand out in a positive way. And it's amazing what people will tell you when you are truly listening to them. People have often said to me, "I can't believe I'm telling you this." And yet, they do tell me very personal things because they perceive that I'm sincerely listening.

Are you listening or waiting to talk?

I heard a story about an American mother and daughter who spent four years as prisoners of war in Japan. The detention camp conditions were deplorable: One third of all prisoners died from beatings, disease or starvation. Prisoners wore rags for clothes and were forced to work at hard labor. The only possessions this mother and daughter had were a two-inch piece of ribbon and a chocolate-chip-sized chunk of lipstick, which they hid from the guards because they believed they would be liberated and wanted to look their best when that time came. When they finally returned to their hometown in California, the mother was asked about her experiences. As she began to explain the difficulties she had been through, the person who asked the question interrupted to tell her how rough it had been in California during that time, and that because gas was rationed they were unable to travel to the Napa Valley to visit their favorite winery. Sadly, the former prisoner vowed then and there that she would never speak of her horrific experiences again because no one was really listening.

Had you been engaged in this conversation, imagine what you could have learned from a firsthand account of what life was like under inhuman conditions. Imagine the healing you could have facilitated by truly listening to someone who experienced such pain. Unfortunately, it is often human nature not to listen. We don't see the importance of our own potential to help others.

The fact is, instead of listening during conversations, people are often just waiting to verbally outdo the other person. This is not only rude; it's counterproductive. If you aren't interested in the comments and stories of others, they are highly unlikely to be interested in yours.

We have all at some point in our lifetime been told to shut up, but I'm willing to bet you've never had anyone tell you to *stop listening*... and you never will. Listening is a powerful and helpful skill, but it takes practice.

Here are some helpful axioms that will help you be a better listener:

- *Just because someone stops talking doesn't mean you should start.* I'll ask someone a pertinent question and will listen to them tell me their answer. When they're done talking, I don't start talking – I'll just keep eye contact with them to let them know that I am truly listening. They may be silent for up to 20 seconds, which may seem like a lifetime, but if I am quiet and maintain eye contact they will usually start speaking again. Except this time, it is at a much deeper and more meaningful level.

- *Just because someone isn't talking doesn't mean they have nothing to say.* Still waters run deep. I have several friends who are very quiet, but once they start talking I just shut up and listen. If you're talking to someone who's going through a crisis, shut up and listen, and avoid giving advice. This is a skill set that requires practice. You don't need to fill dead air – just be quiet and listen.

- *If you take the letters in the word 'listen' and rearrange them, they spell 'silent.'* Being a good listener takes practice and concentration.

- *It's impossible to talk and listen at the same time.* It is also crucial to listen with focus instead of thinking about what your response will be.

- *The listener controls the direction of the conversation.* By asking questions, you as the listener can better understand what someone is trying to tell you. However, once you ask a question, be quiet. This is especially helpful with people who are naturally quiet. Your conversation will go to a whole new level.

When someone is talking to you, ask questions. Stop listening halfheartedly, in black and white. Fill in the color by asking specific questions. Only then will you better understand your fellow human beings and gain knowledge that will enhance your personal and professional relationships.

APPLY THIS IN YOUR LIFE:
The next time you are having a conversation, concentrate on listening and asking thoughtful questions based on what you are hearing. Be truly interested in what the person is telling you. Just because they stop talking doesn't mean you start. Be patient and allow them the opportunity to finish their thought. You will be amazed at how much deeper the conversation will become, and what you will learn about him/her.

Track when you practiced these techniques and how it benefitted you.

_____

_____

_____

_____

_____

_____

_____

_____

_____

_____

_____

_____

About The Author

Being perceived as sincere, energetic and engaging are quintessential characteristics necessary for forming the interpersonal connections that will land you a job, build your business and grow your professional network. Unfortunately, many people don't realize they are being perceived 24/7/365 and that their actions are speaking much louder than their words. You need to hear the truth as to how others perceive you, your actions, your company and your employees, but where can you go to hear the truth?

Donald Wayne McLeod developed PERCEPTIONOLOGY® so you can hear the truth. His unique, informative and entertaining sessions happen in real time as he effectively interacts with his audience members bringing to light certain behaviors he observes while candidly explaining to them how their behavior is being perceived by others, either positively or negatively, ensuring deep learning all along the way. He may not tell you what you want to hear but he will tell you what you need to hear.

High Schools, Colleges and Universities not only bring Donald Wayne in to speak to their students, who are starving for this information realizing their need to separate themselves from the crowd and the importance of building fruit bearing networks, but to work with their faculty, administration and staff as well. Donald Wayne facilitated ten 90 minute voluntary and productive meetings for the Chardon High School faculty, staff and administration during the summer of 2013 to promote open communication and healing after the tragic shooting in 2012.

To give insight into his impactful nature, Donald Wayne presented a two and a half hour lecture to a solemn group of 300 company employees who had suddenly learned their company was moving out of state leaving them all unemployed. Yet he received a heartfelt standing ovation as his personal and caring message not only inspired them but made them feel even more employable and in control of their future moving forward.

After a keynote speech he presented, at a Women's Leadership Conference, Donald Wayne was told that women's restrooms are usually chatty but after hearing his message the restroom was off-the-hook!

Donald Wayne's profound ability to connect with his audience is quite evident as you witness audience members patiently standing in line, sometimes for over an hour, waiting for their opportunity to meet him and receive a PERCEPTIONOLOGY wristband which serves as a daily reminder of the principles presented during his lectures.

Donald Wayne loves what he does because he loves people. If you ever have the opportunity to attend even one of his sessions GO so you can witness firsthand his energy and passion to help others overcome their personal fears, realize their ability to encourage everyone around them and to be the best they can be.

From High Schools to Universities from Fortune 500 to Mom and Pop shops Donald Wayne's message is universal. He will inspire you and your employees to recognize the subtle yet critical nuances that influence others' perceptions. He will teach you how to make a great first impression, present yourself as a true professional and endear yourself to others all the while inspiring others to want to help you achieve your ultimate goals in life.

Donald Wayne McLeod has been featured in Inside-Business Magazine, The Cleveland Plain Dealer, The News-Herald, WEWS Channel 5, WELW and WTOE Radio. To book an event or learn more about Donald Wayne McLeod and PERCEPTIONOLOGY please visit www.PERCEPTIONOLOGY.com

PERCEPTIONOLOGY, LLC
P.O. Box 451
Chardon, Ohio 44024

DonaldWayne@PERCEPTIONOLOGY.com

www.Linkedin.com/in/DonaldWayneMcLeod

Made in USA - Kendallville, IN
915101_9781503056183
01.07.2021 1237